POETIC VOYAGES
BOURNEMOUTH

Edited by Lucy Jeacock

First published in Great Britain in 2001 by
YOUNG WRITERS
Remus House,
Coltsfoot Drive,
Peterborough, PE2 9JX
Telephone (01733) 890066

All Rights Reserved

Copyright Contributors 2001

HB ISBN 0 75433 308 6
SB ISBN 0 75433 309 4

FOREWORD

Young Writers was established in 1991 with the aim to promote creative writing in children, to make reading and writing poetry fun.

This year once again, proved to be a tremendous success with over 88,000 entries received nationwide.

The Poetic Voyages competition has shown us the high standard of work and effort that children are capable of today. It is a reflection of the teaching skills in schools, the enthusiasm and creativity they have injected into their pupils shines clearly within this anthology.

The task of selecting poems was therefore a difficult one but nevertheless, an enjoyable experience. We hope you are as pleased with the final selection in *Poetic Voyages Bournemouth* as we are.

CONTENTS

Christ The King RC Primary School
Hannah McKay	1
Laura Treggiden	1
Sophie Chester	2
Ben Mitchell	3
Sarah Crease	3
Andrew Cooke	4
Michael Barrington	4
Leah Crease	5
Ruth Burgum & Lauren Ofriel	6
Lewis Murphy	6
Kyle Hyde	7
Danniella Reilly	7
Amelia Scott	8
Cecilia Bolt & Caryanne Salmons	8
Joanna Connelly	9
Francesca Runyard	9
Amy Burrows	10
Bianca Baker	11
Alex Hope	12
Charles Lapworth	12
Kyle Greene	12
Levi Hambidge	13
Sinead Smith	13
Natalie Thomas	13
Emma Senior	14
Mariam Kazem-Malaki	14
Jemma Excell	15
Adam Light	15
Danielle Neubauer	16
Sophie Chenery	16

Corpus Christi RC Primary School
Lorraine Conway	16
Jack Higgins	17
William Barry	17

Daniel McQuade	18
Martine McGrath	18
Deanna Sweetland	19
Jenny Heath	20
Christa Hanley	21
Mark Lynch	22
Anthony Ellis	22
Aaron Chavez-Munoz	23
James Emmett	23
Richard Kane	24
Clara Twamley	24
Jasmine Buckmaster	25
Tara Tyszkiewicz	25
Charlotte Gilbert	26
Dannielle Knight	26
Michael Newby	27
Tilly Ingle	27
Stephanie O'Neill	28
Christopher O'Hanlon	28
Tim Ellis	29
Adam Mugan	30
Rose Worrall	31
Alex Caples	32
Natasha Bain	32
Antonio Wellman	33
Alison West	34
Maheva Butchart	34
Callie Emerton	35
Trudie Pavelin	35
Bethany Wentworth	36
Elizabeth Holt	36
Jade Webb	37
Samuel Laidlaw	37
Thomas Horne	38
Olivia Battistini	38
Victoria Cunniffe	39
Ashley Brackstone	40

Celine Bouchex	41
Alex Simpson	42
Amberley Williams	42
Gessica Mancini	43
Melissa Maher	44
Claire Kendall	45
Oliver Simpson	46
Steven Lee	46
Mica Corcoran	47
Rebecca Bright	47
Katie Green	48
Shelley Green	48
Simon Hook	49
Anthony Hughes	49
Edward Roberts	50
Luca Pozzato	50
Conor Mugan	51
Luca Battistini	51
Caitlin O'Grady	52
Sophie Goodhead	52
Megan Evans	53
Tom Barry	53
Michelle Hooper	54
Oliver Duncan	54
Charlotte Grant	55
Carl Mallon	55
Alice Cherry	56
Daniel Quinn	56
Greg Martin	57
Hanna Thiel	58
Oliver Miccoli	58
Anna Gaw	59
Callum MacDermott	60
Yasmin Britton	60
Hannah Dawson	61
Lucy Musgrave	61
Finn Donnelly	62

Alexandra Fellowes	62
James Ethell	63
Samuel Goodman	63
Ryan Chancellor	64
Andrew Clarke	64
Shane Cole	65
Maria-Helena Farah	65
Stephanie Hayden	66
Jade Gardener	66
Hannah Coope	67
Francesca McGrath	68
Yasmin Dow	68
Louis Higgins	69
William Simpson	69
Joshua Hayes	70
Charlotte Smith	70
Michael Gibbons	71
Joseph Shean	71
Roisin Butler	72
Dale Main	72
Christopher Clarke	73
Aidan Rogers	73
Sarah Coleman	74
Martha Nolan	74
Sean Numan	75
Cordelia Wilson-Read	75
Robert Cassell	76
Rachael Grierson	77
Michelle Sherwood	78
Alexandra Burns	78
Alexandra Howarth	79
Camillantonia Mazzeo	79
Natacha Lockyer	80
Peter Mallon	80
Oliver Biles	81
Naomi Ellis	81
Pippa Heath	82

Josh Sherriff	83
James Winyard	84
Madelon van Eerde	85
Sarah Barritt	86
Sam Satchwell	86
Hayley Kennedy	87
Samantha Richardson	88
Kourosh Tehrani	88
Shannon Main	89
Zoe Barber	90
Stephen Bunting	90
Sally Thom	91
Pierangela Marino	91
Daniel Price	92
Daniel Vigar	92
Nicholas Waylett	93
Sean Van Buiten	94
Salvador McCracken	94
Emily Wentworth	95
Jacquetta Bowley	95
Christy O'Grady	96

Heathlands Primary School

Ryan Johnson	96
Melissa Mitchell	97
Laura Ellis	98
Joey Croft	98
Gemma Dean	99
Marc Harris	99
Sophie Harding	100
Craig Biddle	100
Abbie Legg	101
Danyella Croucher	101
Karen Whiting	102
Kurt Barter	102
Jason Coombs	103
Chelsea Jones	104

Stephanie Churchill	104
Chloe Diamond	105
Tanya Brierley & Samantha Waldron	105
Lisa Fitzpatrick	106
Lauren Coat	106

Kingsleigh Junior School

Ryan Balch	106
Stevie Wright	107
Lauren Fox	107
Daniel Ellis	108
Rebecca Charig	108
Charlotte Millett	109
Jennifer Rizza	109
Paul Kim	110
Hannah Moore	110
Marc Crook	111
Martin Vivian	112
Cassie Lazenbury	112
Chloé Hooper	113
Adam Higgins	113
Elizabeth Heron	114
Lee Bartaby	114
Emily Hackin	115
Rosie Dimmer	115
Steven Sheehy	116
Vivienne Henstridge	116

King's Park Primary School

Rachel Innes	117
Molly McCann	117
Portia Criswick	118
Lisa Curtis	118
Amber Wood	119
Christina Bradley	119
Frances Fletcher	120
Fizza Haider	120
Tara Lonnen	121

Mathew Chilton	122
Sunghee Kim	122
Emily Easthope	123
Anna Savage	123
Katy Dimech	124
Elliot Fensom	124
Freya Coles	125
Vanessa Miles	125

St Mark's Primary School

Kristopher Hearsum	126
Jenny Houston	126
Rebecca Brown	127
Jonathan Wheatley	128
Jacob Stanley	128
Luke Granger	129
Oliver Barton	129
Carla Gosling	130
Samantha Reeves	130
James Crotty	131
Sophie Phillips-Pitman	132
Sam Cooper	132
Matthew Gunter	133
Gemma Henry	134
Heather Jardine	134
Jodie Cutler	135
James Appleton	136
Drew Duglan	136
Hannah Boughton	137
Emma Harrison	138
Max Lovell	139
Kiran Patel	139
Oliver Hashtroudi	140
Danielle Lane	140
Brooke Zaidman	141
Kerry Short	142
Thomas Bell	142
Kirsty Chant	143

Melissa Lindsay	144
Marcus Whitmarsh	144
Jack Kane	145
Leah Morgan	146
Chloe Underwood	146
Charlotte Muspratt	147
Matthew Hall	147
Hannah Palmer	148
Matthew Clark	148
Lauren Ostler	149
Alex Barlow	149
Eleanor King	150
Rebecca Airey	150
Verity Younger	151
Philip Watts	152
Jemima Loveys	152
Daniel McIllmurray	153
Lucy Lee	154
Stuart Lucas	154
Lauren Marsh	155
Matthew Downton	156
Callum West	156
Miles Chalkley	157
Georgina Anderson	158
John William Cousin Arias	158
Charlotte Cox	159

St Martin's School

Georgia Vale	159
Darcia George	160
Arvinder Athwal	160
Kristina Guaggenti	161
Alessandro Guaggenti	162
Gabriella Crouch	163
Jayde Morgan	163
Leo Sharer	164
Ben Stanley-Clarke	164
Sarah Shenton	165

Sarah Moneypenny	166
Harri Lawrence	167
Alice Carden	168
Emily Wilson	168
Luke Naveira	169
Hannah Whiteside	170
Leyla MacDonald	170
Lauren Harvey	171
Blue Miller	171
Alex Harvey	172
Lauren Harley	172
Christopher Parsons	173
James Frearson	173

St Thomas Garnet's School

Laura Begeman	174
Samuel Plank	174
Theresa Gillings	175
Tom Weston	175
Brookeleah Gossling	176
Bethany Wildeman	176
Harry Brown	177
Rachel Gillings	177
Rachel Dingley	178
Sam Ring	178
Olivia Johnson	179
Toby Khalife	180
Amy Coppini	180
Liam Cosgrove	181
Philippa King	181
Oliver Porter	182
Isabella Clark	182
Rose Weston	183
Grace Garrett-Sadler	183
Maeve Dunne	184
Jana Browne	184
Laura Johnson	185
Kapil Chauhan	186

Emily King	186
Catherine Hixson	187
Kristy O'Donnell	188
Kamilah Hassan	188
Tom Flynn	189
Connor Rockey	189
Natalie Rondeau	190
Francesca Welsh	190
India Hall	191
George Soan	191
Jamie Rickard	192
Amy Spencer	192
Sophie Skinner	193
Liam O'Leary	194
Todd Lewis	194
Joshua Harris	195
Ross Browne	195

Stourfield Junior School

Disa Daly & Chloe Seaward	196
Bethany Hawker & Georgia McKinney	196
Yasmin Philpott	197
Nick Slumber & Sam Excell	197
Rebekah Oliver	198
Charlotte Ponton & Rudi Barwis	199
Scott Nicol & Adam Salih	200
Amanda Shonfeld	200
Hannah Witcombe	201
Matthew Sloane	202
Rebecca Sheppard	202
Katie Guy	203
Francesca Affleck	203
Jessica Brankin	204
Colin Whittam	205
Claire McGrath	206
Paul Magookin	206
Rosanna Sly	207
Melissa Bailey	207

Sophie Ferguson	208
Patrick Sullivan	209
James Sumner	210
Abbey Murphy	211
Kelly-Anne Conway	212
Naomi Harvey	212
Nicola Crawley	213
Sophie Lankester	214
Stephanie Roy	214
Ryan Carter	215
Jamie Roe	216
Jade Hall	216
Lauren Miller	217
Jake Harvey	218
Nicholas Benavidez	218
Kristy Legg	219
Harry Lund	220
Karen Hawey	220
Alex Winston	221
Zoe Stanley	221
Adam Chastney	222
Gina Legg	223
Liam Coleborn	224
Lewis Gilbert & Ziad Alazhar	224
Simon Challis	225
Rory Lucas	226
Stephanie Gibbons & Roseanna Blackshaw	226
Adam Watt	227
Hannah Godwin	228
Kyle Freeman	230
Ross Hawey	230

The Poems

HOLIDAYS

Holidays in hotness,
Holidays in the cold,
Holidays in places that have stories to be told.

Holidays in jungles,
Holidays in deserts,
Holidays that are way too far away to be measured.

Holidays in ships,
Holidays in planes,
Holidays in cars; jumping all the lanes.

But there's one question that I have
And it's no disgrace:
When will I ever go to space?

Hannah McKay (9)
Christ The King RC Primary School

IS ANYONE THERE?

The traveller knocked on the creaky door,
He had come from huge fields and a very dirty moor.

'I've come to deliver a message for you,
Even though I do not know if it is true'.

The door opens 'Let's go in!'
The traveller gives a great big grin.

Someone gave a loud, loud laugh 'Ha, ha, ha!'
'Oh no, I'm locked in, ahhhhhh!'

Laura Treggiden (9)
Christ The King RC Primary School

THIS WONDERFUL WORLD

There's a love in my life
That is hard to explain,
A light in my heart
That is hard to contain.

The feeling surrounds me
And makes me feel warm,
Cuddling me, holding me,
Always making me calm.

The beauty it carries
Is there for all to see,
It's here in the atmosphere
For all, not just for me.

We'll never feel lonely
When such wonder abounds,
We'll never get bored of it
For it's just so profound.

My love is the wonderful world
We have here,
How we see, talk and listen
It all becomes clear.

God gave us this love,
This life to embrace,
So let's all enjoy it
This world, a wonderful place.

Sophie Chester (10)
Christ The King RC Primary School

THE OLD GRANDFATHER CLOCK

At twelve o'clock
The old grandfather clock
Struck!
There was a man outside looking at me
Suddenly
The window opened,
The door knob turned,
The clock was still ticking,
The curtains were opening,
The light kept going on and off,
Then it all stopped,
The man outside had disappeared.

Ben Mitchell (10)
Christ The King RC Primary School

MY PET DOG

I walked in the shop,
I saw a little puppy
He was fluffy and furry
He felt really soft.

I held out my hand
He lifted his paw
I shook it at once
Then it barked out loud.

I bought that puppy
The puppy that barked
I love my little puppy
And I've called him Fluffy!

Sarah Crease (7)
Christ The King RC Primary School

SWIMMING

Splash went the elephant
Off the diving board.
Bang went the elephant
Landing on the ground.
The bull growled and growled at the cow
Mooo! Went the cow.
Here comes cat, purr she goes.
Let's go get some grub
I'll have a sausage then.
Be careful elephant, he skidded up
Crunch went his bone
Squelch went the chef putting
The food on the plate.

Andrew Cooke (9)
Christ The King RC Primary School

AT THE DEAD OF NIGHT

'Hello, anyone here?
I need a place to stay.'
Suddenly the door opened.
The man walked in trembling;
Lightning struck,
Bones clattered,
A gust of wind
Made windows shake
And curtains fly.
'I'm getting out of here,
Ahhhhhhh!'

Michael Barrington (9)
Christ The King RC Primary School

BIRTHDAY SURPRISE

I wake up one morning
Jump out of bed,
I felt my heart banging
Inside my head!

A big pile of presents
From my mum and dad,
It's going to be the best
Birthday I ever had!

From both my sisters
A beanie or two,
A parcel of clothes which
Are all bright and new!

Wait there's one more
They say,
I wonder if it will
Make my day!

As my excitement grew
Could it be possible,
That my dream
Will come true?

I open the box
Very carefully,
Inside was a sweet bunny
Looking at me!

With sticking up ears and
A wuffling nose,
I love little bunny wherever
He goes!

Leah Crease (10)
Christ The King RC Primary School

My Team Is Not Scoring

It's raining, it's pouring and my team's not scoring
Their goalkeeper's yawning
He could rest his head in the back of the net
And we would still have no chance of scoring.
It's raining, it's pouring now I'm the one that's yawning
No scoring, so boring, no chance of ever scoring
Not raining, nor pouring, not boring, not boring
Now I feel myself snoring
Not raining, nor pouring can you believe my team hasn't been scoring?
Listen to the crowds applauding
. . . Eh! . . . Oh! . . . Eh! . . .
It's raining, it's pouring, now I've just seen my team scoring!

Ruth Burgum (9) & Lauren Ofriel (10)
Christ The King RC Primary School

The Race

And there go the crabs snap!
The giant sea is in the lead
But the river is as fast as a Formula One racing car
And it is burning up the stream
It has overtaken the sea
The furious sea is terrified,
Jagged rocks are in the way
And the sea is in the lead again and they are speeding bullets
But the river has made a terrific come back
And the river has won!

Lewis Murphy (8)
Christ The King RC Primary School

THE BEACH

On a sunny autumn day
A playful cloud took some water and dropped it on a sandcastle
The children stayed wrapped up warm.
The sun came out and the children went to play in the sea,
Ice cream,
Fish and chips,
Fizzy drinks,
Beach balls,
Buckets and spades,
Candyfloss.

Lying bloated in the sun
Smiles on their faces from all the fun.
Kites in the sky fluttering everywhere
Everyone's leaving
The sun's dropping its rays behind the cliffs
It's making the sand go orange
Because it's so hot!

Kyle Hyde (9)
Christ The King RC Primary School

MY FAVOURITE FOOD

My favourite food is spaghetti Bolognese
I like it because it is swirly and yummy!

Well this is hard to believe but my favourite dessert is chocolate cake
That's the part where I stuff my face!

My favourite chocolate bar is an Aero
I like it because of the bubbles inside it.

Danniella Reilly (7)
Christ The King RC Primary School

THE STORM

Crash!
The thunder roared in the grey, cloudy sky
The storm is like a roaring lion
Shaking his mane
Looking out for prey
Quietly he sneaks, then . . .
Crash!
He strikes
The lion is pushing
His way through the dark jungle
Like the wind pushing
In the cold sky.
Striking and hitting what ever it can find.

Amelia Scott (9)
Christ The King RC Primary School

ZOOM!

Zoom! Oh no!
He's at it again!
Growling madly, he's gone for a fight
Bang, bang, bang, 'Oh no don't do that!'
Purring angrily the cat went for revenge.
Splash, 'Benny come here!'
Crunch, 'Oh that was my toe!'
Smack, 'Bad boy
On your bed.'
Oh-oh!

Cecilia Bolt (10) & Caryanne Salmons (9)
Christ The King RC Primary School

WINTER

Winter is a
Cold,
White,
Polar bear throwing down the snow in
Big,
Round,
Balls as big as footballs
Then thrashing rain falls on the
Kind,
Naughty,
Polar bear who walks around on the snow
Making rain with his feet
Finally he lays down and sleeps!

Joanna Connelly (9)
Christ The King RC Primary School

ONOMATOPOEIC POEM

Oh no! He's at it again,
Growling at the cat,
Splash! The dog pushed the cat in the pool,
Oh no! The cow's out of her barn, moo,
Crunch! She's squashed Mum's flowers,
Bang! Go the pots
The horse pushed them over, neigh, neigh,
Oh no! My dad's home!

Francesca Runyard (10)
Christ The King RC Primary School

THE JUNGLE

The jungle is a lonely place with big mahogany trees
With huge, tall leaves
With gigantic ferns going from side to side
In a massive gusty wind
With tropical food like coconuts.

The jungle is open wide to all that live around
The jungle is big with scary animals like
Monkeys,
Tigers,
Leopards,
Snakes,
Bears,
Gorillas,
Lizards
And dragonflies.

You can hear the grasshopper grinding its legs
In the great, big, long grass waiting to be caught
Stag beetles,
Tadpoles,
Baby frogs.

The tiger,
With his clashing teeth and shaggy jaws.
The monkey,
Swings from tree to tree munching on the food outdoors.
The leopard,
Prowling, licking its lips waiting to catch his prey.
The snake,
Slithering around trying not to make a sound.
The bear,
Coming out of his daily sleep very angry with a gleam in his eyes.
The gorilla,
Hitting his greasy chest in anger.
The lizard,
Poking his tongue out every second of the day.

Now you have heard this amazing sound
You'll probably think twice before going into the jungle.
Or you will be sssssssssss
Scared.

Amy Burrows (9)
Christ The King RC Primary School

THE SEASON FIGHT

Hurry it's the season fight
Winter and summer having a fight
Who will win?
Well, summer might.

Summer comes out looking ready with
Flowers,
Sunny spells
And things that are warm.

And in comes winter looking groggy with
Ice cubes,
Snowdrops
And things that are cold.

Ooh! Winter's down for half the count
And it's up.
Summer's down ooh!
It gets up with its shining rays,
The sun is as hot as a lion's mane
The winter is as cold as a polar bear
Time's up!
And winter's down
Summer wins!

Bianca Baker (8)
Christ The King RC Primary School

Sunshine

The sun shines bright
In the morning light.

In the day
So we can play.

On until noon
Then the afternoon.

When we go
We always know.

The sun shines on
For days to come.

Alex Hope (10)
Christ The King RC Primary School

My Best Friend

My best friend he's really cool
He can fly, he's nobody's fool!
He is brainy, full of maths
He has a skateboard, scares the cats!

Charles Lapworth (8)
Christ The King RC Primary School

My Pet Fish

I feed it every day
It blows bubbles every day
It flaps, it flaps, every day!
It gets bigger and bigger every day.

Kyle Greene (7)
Christ The King RC Primary School

SHOES

Shoes go click and shoes go tap!
With shoes you could run a lap!

If you do up your lace
You could be in a race!

If you don't wear shoes
You might lose!

Levi Hambidge (8)
Christ The King RC Primary School

SNOWFLAKES

Snowflakes falling down from the sky,
Look, look they are so beautiful up high
Let's go out for a snowflake fight,
I got hit,
Mum tell him off
Not really.

Sinead Smith (7)
Christ The King RC Primary School

DRIP, DROP, PLOP

Drip, drop, plop
Went the big raindrop
Mummy said we might have to use a mop
We hope it stops
We want to go to the shops.

Natalie Thomas (10)
Christ The King RC Primary School

SOME THINGS ABOUT NATURE

The river is as transparent as a glass bottle
It is as fresh as a newborn baby
It is very lovely in summer.

The sea is as fierce as a boxer
Sometimes in winter the waves are as big as mountains.

Spring is as lovely as a queen
Spring is as colourful as an artist's palette.

Summer is as hot as the sun
Clouds are as rare as a purple horse
(Sometimes).

In autumn the leaves are as colourful as a rainbow.

Winter is as white as a snow leopard
It is as cold as an iceberg.

Emma Senior (8)
Christ The King RC Primary School

EARTHQUAKE

My heart beats boom - boom
The ground shook, it cut in half,
The homes break and also the towers.
I looked then I fell to the ground
Next I was being pulled out of my home
My family was being pulled out too
The earthquake went in a minute.

Mariam Kazem-Malaki (8)
Christ The King RC Primary School

MY BIRTHDAY

I wake up in the morning
And had a big surprise
To see all my presents wrapped
Up on one side.

I opened them up
And was very happy!
I had a dog
I will name him Yappy.

I got clips, clothes, toys
And a little toy car
That makes a weird noise.

I had a few friends
Round to have a cool party
And some lovely food.

But then all my friends
Have to go
So I get in a big mood.

Damn it, time for bed
Well that was my birthday.

Jemma Excell (10)
Christ The King RC Primary School

TIME

It's funny, it's fast
It really, really flies!

Oh gosh, I'm already late for school!
I just wish I had more time!

Adam Light (8)
Christ The King RC Primary School

SNOWFLAKES

Snowflakes, snowflakes
Falling down,
Snowflakes, snowflakes
On the ground,
Snowflakes, snowflakes
On the ground
We play with snowflakes
Snowflakes, snowflakes
All around!

Danielle Neubauer (8)
Christ The King RC Primary School

MY PETS

I have a pet
And it's a cat
And I have a dog
My dog chases
My cat and the cat
Jumps over me
My mum she goes mad
My pets!

Sophie Chenery (8)
Christ The King RC Primary School

MY PET

My pet is very naughty
She went to the park alone
She left me on my own
I'd rather give her a bone.

My pet is very naughty
She never eats her dinner
She always wants to play
She clings to my sister every day.

Lorraine Conway (7)
Corpus Christi RC Primary School

The Site

The tools are running,
The hammers are talking,
The mallets are fizzing,
The tape measures are rolling,
The tool box is jittering,
The rulers are smothering,
The workers are slacking,
The desk lids are opening,
The desk lids are closing.

Jack Higgins (7)
Corpus Christi RC Primary School

The Ghost

There once was a ghost
Who loved to eat toast
And was a little bit grumpy
But the worst thing of all
His head was too small
And his face was a little bit lumpy.

William Barry (8)
Corpus Christi RC Primary School

SPACE

The sun sets in the west
The sun that's big, it's the best
The sun floats out in deep space
It lets us live the human race.

The Earth it orbits round the sun
All astronomy it is fun
The moon it orbits round the Earth
The moon looks at it, it has a curve.

All the planets and the stars
Especially the moon and Mars
And the galaxy it is there
So if you're travelling then beware.

Saturn, Jupiter, Pluto and Mars
Are planets and also stars
Way up high they shine so bright
Sometimes you'll think it wasn't night.

Daniel McQuade (10)
Corpus Christi RC Primary School

WHEN I WENT TO THE BEACH

When I went to the beach,
I went into the sea
And when I got out
I got stung by a bee.

When I went to the beach
I went into the sea
And when I got out
I ate a pea.

When I went to the beach
I drank lemonade
And when I finished
I dug with my spade.

When I went to the beach
I went into the sea
And guess what I saw?
A bumblebee!

Martine McGrath (11)
Corpus Christi RC Primary School

ANIMALS

Animals come in all sizes
Big and small
Thin and fat
I even saw a dog three feet tall.

Cats are cute
And dogs are scruffy
Some animals are
Really fluffy.

I saw a girl
Walking a bunny
My mum thought
It was really funny.

There was this hare
He was just standing there
Next to a
Eight foot bear.

Deanna Sweetland (9)
Corpus Christi RC Primary School

THE RABBIT

I can see it now,
A blackened shape hopping towards me
Eyes warm and welcoming,
Like a cup of tea on a cold night.

Its whiskers twitching,
Nose sniffing the air.
It stops to nibble the grass
And gazes at the gold trees
Shimmering in the sunlight.

Now it's coming towards me
Racing like a car
Its ears pulled back
By the wind.

Paws thudding on the grassy hill,
It lifts its head towards the sun.
It looks around cautiously,
Then thud, it comes down
On all fours.

It takes off like a bolt of lightning
And reaches a hole.
As quick as a flash
It darts into the hole
And never comes to breathe
Fresh air again.

Jenny Heath (11)
Corpus Christi RC Primary School

A Witch's Spell

Hubbly bubbly, bubble and crack
Scary Mary, big dead cat
Leary cary green frog's eye
Teary darey you small fly.

The big cauldron big and black
Heavy and small like a rat
There's a dead man's toe on the spoon
When you look up at the moon.

All the bottles green and blue
Don't drink them you'll get a flu,
In the potion is a grey hair
Oh come on that's not fair.

In goes a spider web out of the corner of the shelf
Don't eat it, it will ruin your health,
Next goes in a squeaky mouse
Quick grab it, it's on the corner shelf.

In goes the horse out of the dirty woods
And the eye out of the big, brown hoods
Get the water out of the lake
And don't forget to kill the snake.

Cut the head off and take out the eye
In the cupboard is a baby fly,
Hubbly bubbly, bubble and crack
Scary Mary, big dead cat.

Christa Hanley (10)
Corpus Christi RC Primary School

MY SISTER AND THE TELLY

My sister Kelly always watches telly
I think my mum and dad made a mistake in the name
I think they should call her Telly not Kelly.

She always lies on the couch
With the telly control on her belly
I like to hide behind the couch
With a spare telly control and keep turning off the telly.

I like to play practical jokes on her
Then me and my family all break out laughing.

At around five o'clock we pretend the telly is broken
By turning off the power
She breaks out crying 'No fix the telly'.

Then she runs upstairs to try her telly
Hoping it will work
Ha, ha!

Mark Lynch (10)
Corpus Christi RC Primary School

HAPPY SIGHTS

Look at that stunning sea washing, twinkling blue and white miniature waves onto the golden beach.
Look at that rare golden bird gliding over a beautiful exotic pine tree in the orange and yellow sunrise.
Look at that chocolate being made dripping and running into the delicious chocolate pot
Look at that . . .

Anthony Ellis (11)
Corpus Christi RC Primary School

IT'S ONLY A GAME

'Shoot, shoot, shoot'
Said the manager to the player.
'Miss, miss, miss'
Yelled the opponent.
How difficult this game of football can be.
Must watch the offside but
Have to get the ball past the keeper into the net.

I must shoot, shoot, shoot
No matter what, but what if I
Miss, miss, miss
The defender stays by my side
Like a shadow on a sunny day.

Now here is my chance to get us in the
Lead, lead, lead.
I outrun my shadow, and take a shot at goal.
The ball glided into the back of the net.
A cheer emptied from the side.

Aaron Chavez-Munoz (11)
Corpus Christi RC Primary School

HALF PAST THREE

I love half past three cos it's time for tea
I love half past three cos Dad bounces Joe upon his knee
But most of all the reason why my favourite time is half past three
The school bell rings and out we run!

James Emmett (8)
Corpus Christi RC Primary School

WAR IS TERRIBLE

War is just conjuncted arguments
No more than punches and fights,
Generals ordering soldiers about
And plundering at the sight
Until the point until it thunders in every state
And shelterless place
People should just think about the homeless and the sick
Instead of thinking about ourselves
And what we've got and what we haven't got.
The influence they give and set
And you shudder to think about it
The KF7 Soviets that bang, boom and wallop
The ferocious sound of war,
And the howling of bombers awaiting their fate.

Richard Kane (11)
Corpus Christi RC Primary School

MY CAT

My cat brings in mice
So if you are prepared to get a cat
Here's my advice
Think before you get one, why not a rat?
You will have to pay a vet bill
If your cat gets ill!
On the night of the fireworks
Keep your cat in
Or you will find your cat will go crazy
And its head will spin.

Clara Twamley (7)
Corpus Christi RC Primary School

My Little Sister

My sister says I'm two
But I say it back to her too.
My sister is such a pest
Because when I have my dinner she eats the rest.
My little sister drives me crazy
Because she is so lazy.
When I come home from school
She wants to play with me all day
So I say
'I do not want to play today'.
At bedtime my sister is so bad
Because she drives me mad.
And that is my little sister.

Jasmine Buckmaster (8)
Corpus Christi RC Primary School

It's Not My Fault

'It's not my fault' said the girl
Around the corner.
'It's not my fault' said the squirrel
In the park.
'It's not my fault' said the pig
In the farm.
'It's not my fault' said the cow
In the field.
And 'It's not our fault' said the people
In the street.

'It's not my fault'.

Tara Tyszkiewicz (11)
Corpus Christi RC Primary School

My Dog

My dog is very lazy
Sometimes he drives me crazy
But when he hears the lead
You'll find he's there.
He never gets up unless
You tell him
But when a piece of chicken is dropped on the floor
You'll find he's there right away.
But I still think he's a great pet
I've had him since he was a puppy
If you ever see him be careful he gets carried away
You should see him at home
He's such a pickle
He's a great pet!

Charlotte Gilbert (7)
Corpus Christi RC Primary School

My Family

My mum and dad
They drive me mad
They tell me off when I'm not doing anything wrong.
In the morning mum says
'Get out of bed you lazy bones'
I say to mum 'I'm awake, you woke up
Connor and Eamonn, that's for sure.'
She awakes Connor, he starts crying out,
He wakes up Eamonn, he gets on my nerves.

Dannielle Knight (8)
Corpus Christi RC Primary School

SPACE!

You know S. P. A. C. E?
It's a very big place!
It has little silver dots
And life forms with very big spots!

You know the *universe*?
If you get lost in it you will curse.
Inside the universe there are lots of planets
And if you are a scientist you will love it!

You know *man*?
They often eat from a can!
They keep pets like cats and dogs
And they have wild animals like foxes and hedgehogs.

Michael Newby (10)
Corpus Christi RC Primary School

MY CRAZY BIRTHDAY

My birthday is lots of fun
We bake a cake one by one,
We eat popcorn and chocolate too
When we get scared we go to the loo!
We go downstairs
And we play musical chairs
And we say 'How do you do?'
We play lots of games
It is very fun
We sit by the phone
And dial 911.

Tilly Ingle (8)
Corpus Christi RC Primary School

THE DREAM

I woke from my dream
Weeping, mournful children, helpless on streets of terror.
The sky hazy grey with morning mist, like a cold wet blanket
Wrapping itself around them.
Children lay barely alive, hunger taking over mind and body
I wandered down the street, glancing fretfully at all I saw.
I felt helpless, nothing to offer, as a child looked longingly at me.

I followed fearful of what the skinny girl would show me.
I felt I was one of the children soon to die of hunger.
We walked through the shanty town,
I saw children weeping,
Some even lying dead.
I thought I would collapse.
I had to stop 'No more,' I shouted.

Tears were dripping from my eyes like a waterfall
Children surrounded me
I couldn't leave them having given them nothing.
I had to stay.
Die with them, feel their pain.
Children were comforting me
'No' I wailed.
I should be the one comforting them
'Noooo . . .'
I woke from my dream.

Stephanie O'Neill (11)
Corpus Christi RC Primary School

WHAT I THINK ABOUT FLOWERS

Flowers are beautiful, flowers are colourful
Flowers are fresh and flowers are just right
To gleam in my back garden
In the middle of the night.

Flowers have a smell of a high quality perfume
That fills the air so there is something there
I love flowers when they grow in the sun and rain
I don't like them much when they are dead and there is nothing there.

Christopher O'Hanlon (10)
Corpus Christi RC Primary School

THE ENVIRONMENT AROUND THE WORLD

The frogs and the toads, jumping and jumping
The trees and the bushes, swaying and swaying,
The plants and the flowers, growing and growing,
The pond and the grass, being smothered with frogs.

The frogs and the toads getting out of the pond
Jumping and jumping to get to the grass
Meeting all the other frogs and toads in the fields
Making sure he doesn't tread on any glass.

The trees and the bushes coping with all sorts of rain
Waiting and waiting for the farmer to come again
Then a farmer came out to plant some seeds
And then he went to give some water to the plants.

The plants and the flowers as huge as a tree
Growing and keep on growing, then he said
'You beautiful plants, you beautiful flowers
The sun will shine on you always'.

The grass in the fields being cut by farmers
The farmers planting all the seeds
The seeds growing into flowers and plants
All in the grass, in the fields.

Tim Ellis (10)
Corpus Christi RC Primary School

Mr Cruel

Teachers at our school
Are extremely uncool,
Especially Mr Cruel.

He burst the eardrums of a boy called Jim,
By screaming, yelling and shouting at him.
He hit a pupil in our year,
For telling him he had big ears.
Now he's yelling at other teachers,
For suggesting a day trip to some beaches.

Teachers at our school
Are extremely uncool,
Especially Mr Cruel.

The pupils thought their only choice,
Was to make their teacher lose his voice.
They would make the teacher shout all day,
So eventually his voice would go away.
This extremely clever plan,
Was formulated by a boy called Dan.

Teachers at our school
Are extremely uncool,
Especially Mr Cruel.

The children all went wild and berserk,
And soon their plan began to work.
This made their teacher shout some more,
And soon his throat was really sore.
Mr Cruel resigned the very next day,
Now all the children can laugh and play.

Teachers at our school
Are extremely uncool,
But at least there's no more Mr Cruel.

Adam Mugan (11)
Corpus Christi RC Primary School

MY LUCKY LEAF

I saw a leaf dancing on a twig
It fell, it was red, green and blue.
I called it my lucky leaf,
I put it in my pocket
I took it inside,
Hid it away.
Then one year later it was golden
I was amazed
I shouted 'I have a magic leaf!'

Rose Worrall (9)
Corpus Christi RC Primary School

A Fishy Tale

I wondered whether my friends did see,
The hooks that dangle in the sea,
They seem so far but yet so near
My heart began to scream with fear.

I do hope my best pals did not suffer,
But unlike me, they are much, much tougher,
They may have bodies as hard as steel,
But they are helpless to the power behind the reel.

Now all alone, cramped up in this bowl,
I shall never achieve my ultimate goal
To swim with my mate - old Freddy the Skate,
But my fate was decided - I ate the bait.

What is out there? I wondered inside,
If I made the big jump, would I be filled with much pride,
Should I be known as Amazo-fish
Or could I end up on a cat's plastic dish?

The truth is out there - for everyone to see,
I am stuck all alone, no one here but me.
Round and round my life is mundane
Is it just me - or am I going insane?

Alex Caples (11)
Corpus Christi RC Primary School

About My Hamster

My hamster is mad
He rolls around and touches the ground
He likes nuts and apples
For breakfast, lunch and dinner
He likes people holding him and stroking him.

If he wakes you up in the night
He is on his wheel.
When it's morning you get up
And might hear him still up.

Natasha Bain (7)
Corpus Christi RC Primary School

NATURE

I love nature with the beautiful lush green grass,
With the lovely bright stars shining down on the brown deer.
The blue sky with nothing in it accept the birds flying around.

You look around, all you can see is snow-capped mountains
And all the animals of the Earth running around free
The fields are yellow with corn and all the blues of the tulips growing.

The trees swaying in the mighty wind,
And in the winter, the fields and the lush grass and the trees
Are covered in white snow,
But if you are lucky you might see a rabbit with a fur coat.

I find it relaxing in the snow but everything is dull,
There are not many animals and no creatures
But when it warms up everything is lovely again
All the apples are sparkling in the sun.

If you go on a boat and jump in
The gorgeous blue sea and swim with dolphins
And you could see the largest mammal in the world
The whale.

When you get home you can still see nature
Out of the window.

Antonio Wellman
Corpus Christi RC Primary School

MY WONDERFUL BEDROOM

In my bedroom I have lots of toys,
I never play with those boys,
On the door there are dolls,
And little green trolls!

I have to tidy my bedroom once a week,
It's a great place to play hide-and-seek,
I have a great big, white bear
My friends say they like to play truth or dare!

In my bedroom I have a big pink light,
My light is very bright,
I have six small drawers,
And two blue doors.

Alison West
Corpus Christi RC Primary School

MY LITTLE SISTER

My little sister
Drives me crazy
Never stops talking
Keeps on chattering
Pulls my hair
Her name is Tonia
I call her Wonyer.
She draws on my homework
Oh I just hate that Wonyer.
My little sister
Drives me crazy.

Maheva Butchart (8)
Corpus Christi RC Primary School

HAUNTED HOUSE

Once there was a haunted house
On the door I knocked
I could hear weird noises but nobody was there
I tried the door, but I found it was blocked
Somebody was behind me but I heard it in the air.

Sunday has turned time to meet a ghost,
It came up to me and said boo hoo
Down by the town I saw some post
The small ghost got bigger and bigger till it grew.

I ran and ran till I found a drive
The huge ghost found me so I ran
I said to the ghost 'Why aren't you alive?'
'I don't know, I used to be a man'.

Callie Emerton (9)
Corpus Christi RC Primary School

MY ROBOTIC DOG, TEXSTA

I love my dog Texsta
Even though he barks a lot!
He follows me everywhere
Like a little tot!
He wakes up in the night
And gives me quite a fright
He does the most amazing tricks
And hides under the sheets!
But you should see at breakfast time
He keeps running away!

Trudie Pavelin (8)
Corpus Christi RC Primary School

My Pet

I live in the country far out west
I watch the sun when it's at its best.

When the sun starts to set,
I start to think about my pet.

It smells like a flower and hums like a bee
It's the greatest pet in history.

It's as large as a tree and as small as a mouse,
It always comes back for tea at my house.

It's the kind of pet your friends adore,
When it's tired it curls up on the floor.

My pet's name is Geraldine,
It hates the smell of margarine.

My pet is so special it's warm and lovely,
My pet's a secret only tell people secretly.

Bethany Wentworth (10)
Corpus Christi RC Primary School

Caterpillars

Caterpillars are green and long
They crawl around all day long.

When they're ready they go in to a nest,
For ages and ages to get some rest.

Then one day they break free,
Flying away as a butterfly happily!

Elizabeth Holt (9)
Corpus Christi RC Primary School

THE GLITTERY SNOW

The glittery snow
I think I will do a snow show
In the heavy and low temperature I sew with snow
Snow is sparkling here and there
Here and there and everywhere
Stop! Help! I'm falling right under.

Tomorrow morning it will be melted
I am really sheltered
I see where it sparkles
Right on top
I think I'm going to freeze to death
That's me, I'm freezing and I'm left.

Sparkle, sparkle everywhere
Oh! I see something what's there?
Sparkle, sparkle here and there and sparkle everywhere
Snow falling down and drifting
I do wish it was lifting
Waaaahhhhhhooooo.

Jade Webb (10)
Corpus Christi RC Primary School

WINTER

W is for white, houses and hills are covered
I is for ice, the fishes live under,
N is for nature, the rain and the thunder,
T is for trickle, in which the snow floats in
E is for explosion, they throw a snowball thin,
R is for ringing at Christmas the church bells ring.

Samuel Laidlaw (10)
Corpus Christi RC Primary School

MOUNTAINS

I was in the snowy mountains
The air was thin and fresh,
I breathe once again
As I prepare for the undertaking moment.

Whoosh! As I slide down the mountains,
Taking a good look at the magnificent sight
I was going slow, I could feel the snow
Beneath my feet.

I eventually reached the bottom,
I felt all tingly inside,
I felt I was the top man as I conquered the mountain
I rushed to the lift again to start all over.

Thomas Horne (10)
Corpus Christi RC Primary School

MY LITTLE SISTER

My little sister is so mad
And then she is so bad
Like this . . .
She plays in the mud
And runs around in the grass
Then she runs in and out of the pond
Like a frog
I don't like her
Very much
She is mad.

Olivia Battistini (8)
Corpus Christi RC Primary School

SONG OF THE MERMAIDS

They swim and slide into the glade
Their tails of rubies, emeralds and jade
Their hair of silver, silk and gold,
Their voices tell of secrets untold.

The sea around them glints and shines,
The treasures greater than from any mine
The palace high and grand and rich
Exquisite foods on a patterned dish.

The fish and dolphins swim around
Happier animals than any found
The carriage waiting for themselves
Pulled by wonderful deep blue whales.

And then they reached their magnificent goal
The entrance a dark and deep black hole
Although the entrance may be dreary,
The party certainly is merry.

For the mermaids laugh and sing
And win the prize for no sin
But for the last and weird guest,
Mischief, badness and cruelness are best.

For though she seems happy enough,
She plots to kill and steal all she thinks is to be rough
The heroes still think she's changed her ways
But they'll lose in a bet, all they've paid
When they find out of their foe,
Of all things she'll boldly go
And just in the nick of time
They save the sea from a terrible crime.
That's the end of the mermaid's song
Whatever you think, it is not wrong.

Victoria Cunniffe (11)
Corpus Christi RC Primary School

SAILING OUT TO SEA

I went sailing on the sea
I got bitten by a flea
The sun was shining on me.
I went sailing on the sea
The storm came later
So did the alligator.
I went sailing on the sea.

I went sailing on the sea
The sun was boiling
Like my tea.
I went sailing on the sea
The rough waves raging
When I was shaving.
I went sailing on the sea.

I went sailing on the sea
I was so hungry I could eat a pea
But I couldn't eat a flea.
I went sailing on the sea
The storm got worse
It broke Mum's purse.
I went sailing on the sea.

I went sailing on the sea
I ate the tiny dirty pea
But did not eat that flea.
I went sailing on the sea
The sinking boat
I wish it would float.

Ashley Brackstone (10)
Corpus Christi RC Primary School

IT GOES ON FOREVER

One day my mum
Said it was time I begun,
The school down the lane,
Which was a pain,
So off I went
With some paper and a pen
After all I was ten,
It went on forever,
Until that is I caught a fever,
So I got to stay home,
In some bubbly foam,
Of a nice hot bath.

Two days after,
There was no laughter,
I had to go back to school,
I'd had enough,
So I started to puff,
I gathered up some patches,
And some matches,
And set off to cause havoc.
At the end of the day,
In the middle of May,
The school was burnt down,
And I thought I deserved the most precious crown.

So with it on my head,
I saw a path that led,
So with a grin on my face,
I started to race,
But I didn't realise that it . . .
Don't tell me, it goes on forever!

Celine Bouchex (10)
Corpus Christi RC Primary School

FOOTBALL CRAZY

My name is Alex
I love playing football
I get very dirty and very smelly
I scored a goal! Oh no! It didn't count.

One day I went to play a football game
I didn't know any of the players names
I went to score a goal
Oh no! The ref had blown his whistle.

'Foul' said the ref.
I got the blame
I had to sit on the sideline
'It's not fair' I said.

After the game
I had a hot bath
We all jumped in
It was a good laugh.

Alex Simpson (10)
Corpus Christi RC Primary School

ANNOYING PROBLEMS AT SCHOOL

I go to Corpus Christi School
It has a deep, light, blue pool,
It is never hot but it is cool,
And I always do my maths.

My friend always likes to moan
But I like to shout 'Let's call'
The boys all like to play ball,
And the teachers can all drink tea.

I love to do write ups,
We have a litter of pups,
We all drink from cups,
And the teachers all eat biscuits.

Why do teachers shout?
There is no need to shout,
The odd thing is they talk about court,
But do teachers neeeeeeeed to shout?

Amberley Williams (10)
Corpus Christi RC Primary School

THE DOLPHIN

The dolphin swims on top of a wave
It doesn't live or seek in a cave
The poor dolphin is there lonely and sad
And they all treat him so bad.

The starfish saw the lonely thing
With his nice soft body down he goes diving
He swims down to sea and meet some fish
With his surprise he even found a dish.

He was so scared to meet them
While he was going he saw a plant with a very long stem
Oh dear, oh dear he bumped his head
Until he went to bed.

The little poor dolphin had nothing to do
Until the other had gone too
He sent a box, a brown box
He opened it up and found a small magical ox.

Gessica Mancini (11)
Corpus Christi RC Primary School

WAKE UP!

I woke up in bed,
With a drowsy head,
Not wanting to go to school.
I clung to my pillow,
And scrunched in a ball,
Awaiting the dreaded call.

I turned to look at the time,
But what was the point,
I knew it was 6.59.
The alarm clock rang,
The morning birds sang,
Oh why is it 6.59?

I heard footsteps coming nearer,
Images of school getting clearer,
As I lay in bed,
With horrid thoughts in my head,
My peaceful night,
Was nearly over!

Have I done my homework right?
I'd done it quickly last night,
Suddenly someone opened my door,
It scared me so much,
I fell out on the floor!

    Wake up!

Melissa Maher (10)
Corpus Christi RC Primary School

ONE EXCITING DAY

Look at that bird
Soaring high in the sky,
It looks absurd
As it performs a dive.

The cats pounce,
As the birds aim for a worm,
Not weighing an ounce,
As it tries to squirm.

Loop the looping in great awe,
At the sight of the undergrowth,
Looking through an open door,
Swaying to and fro.

Gliding through the empty sky,
Seeing the whole world,
Sliding past a pig sty,
Feeling a bit bored.

Finding its nest at last,
Swallowing the worm,
Decreasing its grasp,
Becoming less and less firm.

Drifting off to sleep,
Tucking its head under its wing,
Not taking a peep,
As it shapes into a ring.

Claire Kendall (10)
Corpus Christi RC Primary School

AT NIGHT-TIME

At night-time
When the ghosts come out
To scare us all
And make us shout.

They flew to the window
And came through the wall
And said to me
That I looked very small.

I ran down the stairs
But they followed me all the way
In the kitchen and on the chairs
They just wouldn't go away.

I ran down the hall
And hurt my knee
The ghosts were coming
But it didn't bother me.

Oliver Simpson (11)
Corpus Christi RC Primary School

THE RIVER

The river is bendy,
It twirls around,
But when it floods,
It makes a lot of sound.

When the river is watered,
With muddy wet rain,
Then it says,
'Yucky yuck, I hate this muddy rain'.

Steven Lee
Corpus Christi RC Primary School

UNTITLED

Down behind the dustbin
I met a pig called Lin
No one would believe me
But she made a real din!

Down behind the dustbin
I met a pig called Kim
He didn't know me
And I didn't know him.

Down behind the dustbin
I met a pig called Jim
He said he was clever
But he looked quite dim!

Mica Corcoran (9)
Corpus Christi RC Primary School

COUNTRY

Rain falls anywhere,
Any day or month,
It doesn't care,
Rain falls anywhere.

Foxes go in your litter bins,
Throwing all the tins,
Foxes go out hunting
In the middle of the night.

Flowers dance from side to side
Dancing around so much and opening
Out really, really, really wide.

Rebecca Bright (9)
Corpus Christi RC Primary School

MY HORSE

My horse called Zoe, is a mare
She has sparkling grey hair
So silky is her mane
Against it lies the rein
She has a long bushy tail
It is as shiny as hail
She has a friend called Mabel
That lives in a stable.
Mabel is always out on a ride
'What about me?' Zoe cried
Zoe instead eats lots of food
It always puts her in a good mood
Zoe is my very best mate
As a friend she is really great.

Katie Green (9)
Corpus Christi RC Primary School

MY CAT

I have a cat
Who is very fat
She likes to eat lots of fish
We put it in her favourite dish
She likes to creep around the house
Maybe she's looking for a mouse
She's soft with very thick fur
To speak she tends to purr
During the day she likes to sleep,
At night she hunts in the forest deep.

Shelley Green (9)
Corpus Christi RC Primary School

I'M A POET AND I DON'T KNOW IT

'Write a poem' my teacher said
Who put that idea in his head?
Poetry is not my thing
I really think I'd rather sing
No more than thirty lines we're told
Ten words later and my brain's on hold.
My thoughts are frozen ideas won't come
Sitting here I feel so glum.
I'm sure Mr Scott would be quite sad,
If he knew I felt so bad
Whoops he hates the word sad,
He'll probably get really mad
'Buy a Thesaurus' he will say
Then I'll write poems every day.
I'll write one for my mum
I'll write one for the cat
I'll be so busy writing poetry
I might forget my SATs!

Simon Hook (11)
Corpus Christi RC Primary School

MESSY MABEL

This is the tale of Messy Mabel
She's not very nice at the kitchen table
When her friends come round for tea
She eats her meats and out she spits her peas.
Now her friends don't come round for tea
She sits on her own and watches TV
Poor Messy Mabel on her own,
Poor Messy Mabel on her own.

Anthony Hughes (8)
Corpus Christi RC Primary School

THE CANDLE OF THE SEA

As the candle sits in front of me,
It waves from side to side,
As we sail upon the deep, blue sea,
Away we seem to glide.

As the candle sits in front of me,
It flickers in the moonlight,
Upon the deep blue sea,
In front of me.

As the candle sits in front of me,
The stars shine brightly,
Reflecting on the sea,
Silently we blow out the candle,
And say goodnight to thee.

Edward Roberts (10)
Corpus Christi RC Primary School

THE BOY WHO LOVED CHOCOLATE

He dreams about chocolates
He thinks about chocolates
This boy, Tom, even went up to space
He found a planet
He then put the flag down
He named it Chocolate World
Now you see why he called it Chocolate World
When you go there you can eat anything
You can eat the ground,
You can eat the trees,
You can eat the clouds,
Would you like to go there?
I would!

Luca Pozzato (8)
Corpus Christi RC Primary School

THE MAN FROM ALACAZAR

There was once a young man from Alacazar
He went to Britain and bought a car
He thought it was cool
But it ran out of fuel
So he went home and cried to his Ma.

Because his car ran out of fuel
He ran straight to the swimming pool
He filled it with water
Then his car shrunk shorter
And now it's as slow as a mule.

'Oh no' he said, 'I'm going to be late
It's time to go shopping, it's a quarter past eight'
So he ran off with a hop
And he found the right shop
And bought himself new roller skates.

Conor Mugan (9)
Corpus Christi RC Primary School

SHOES

Tip tap, tip tap, tip tap, toe
On the floor my shoes will go
Tip tap, tip tap, tip tap, click
Back together they will stick
Tip tap, tip tap, tip tap slide
On the floor I will glide
All around me the crowd cheer as I pirouette in the air
Down to the ground I drop with a very gentle plop
As I take my final bow the crowd around me just go 'Wow'
All around me down they shower big bunches of bright flowers.

Luca Battistini (11)
Corpus Christi RC Primary School

MY NEW HOUSE

My new house is very old,
It's creepy, quiet but the sign says sold!
When we pulled up at the broken gate,
My dad said great, but I thought hate!

The kitchen is so very cold,
Most of all there's loads of mould.
The ceiling it is falling in
My dad came to the rescue with a very big bin!

The garden is so very big,
It's hard to find Sally when we're playing tig
Also there's a big, wet pond,
With my favourite frog, we're very fond!

My new room is best of all
It's yellow to match my cupboard so tall
I also like my bouncy bed,
To jump around with my teddy Ted!

I suppose it's really not that bad,
But it still gets me really mad!

Caitlin O'Grady (10)
Corpus Christi RC Primary School

THE SWAPPING POEM

I went to the cook and gave her a book
She gave me a mat
I gave it to the cat
The cat gave me a rat
Oh boy! That rat was fat.

Sophie Goodhead (8)
Corpus Christi RC Primary School

AT THE BEACH

At the beach I have plenty of fun,
While my mum is dozing in the sun.
I splash in the sea and build in the sand,
I have a good time, it is really grand.

One day on the beach I met my friend Paul
He's a very good swimmer and best at front crawl.
We like to play with a bouncy beach ball,
And the hours pass in no time at all.

The sea sparkles and shines and reflects the light,
But now it's coming up to night.
I'll soon have to go away from this perfect day,
Pick up my things and be on my way.

I will come back to the beach again,
But now we're having lots of rain.
Maybe tomorrow the sun will come out,
And I'll be back on the beach without a doubt!

Megan Evans (8)
Corpus Christi RC Primary School

THE SHARK

The shark's jaws sharper than the silver knife
Get out the water or it will take your life
Its shimmering eyes flash in the sun
If it sees you his job will be done.

Snap, snap, snap goes its threatening teeth
If it sees you in the ocean it will bite from underneath
The killing machine acts unlike an animal
Eating the innocent, mammal to mammal.

Tom Barry (10)
Corpus Christi RC Primary School

Spawn

Spawn, spawn we all know
The stages of spawn
It starts like this . . .

Stage one: the spawn
Floats like eggs
With a little black yoke
In the middle.

Stage two: a tadpole
Well they are just a little body all
Black with a tail then
Legs, long legs.

Stage three: a frog
It has big black legs
Sometimes a big mouth
So that's the stages of spawn.

Frogs, frogs . . .

Michelle Hooper (10)
Corpus Christi RC Primary School

My Crazy Guy

I have a cue and its colour is blue
Someone said 'It's time for bed'
I knew he has a cue but it was not blue
'Who is this guy?' I said
Someone said 'His name is Mr Bed'
I said 'Mr Bed! I would have called him Mr Head!'
I said to Mr Bed
'Mr Crazy Head!'

Oliver Duncan (7)
Corpus Christi RC Primary School

WAVES

As the waves crash
Into the pier
The surfers surf
Up here.

Catch the waves
The wind is blowing
In my hair
The winter's breeze
Chills my spine.

How could they do that?
My, oh my
I couldn't do that
If I tried and tried
They must be amazing
I surely think they are.

Charlotte Grant (9)
Corpus Christi RC Primary School

MY WEEK

On a Saturday I play football
Sunday I sing in a church hall.
On a Monday I go to school,
Tuesday I go to the swimming pool.
Wednesday I don't act the fool,
I do my homework after school.
Thursday I play with the mouse,
On the computer in my house.
Friday is my favourite date,
As I get to stay up late.

Carl Mallon (8)
Corpus Christi RC Primary School

IN BED

When I'm sent to bed at night,
Up I go without a fight,
All the darkness and the gloom,
So off I go to my room.

When I'm in my bed at night,
All that darkness is a fright,
On my pillow I lay my head,
I love my lovely warm bed.

When it is late at night,
I look into the hall full of light,
I shut my tired eyes to sleep,
It's so quiet not a peep.

Then when everyone's asleep,
There I am counting sheep,
In the morning when it's light,
It will be all right.

Alice Cherry (10)
Corpus Christi RC Primary School

THE TEN MILE MONSTER

There once was a monster
Who stretched for ten miles.
His feet were very smelly
And he never ever smiled.

One day I found him
Starting to cry.
He'd lost his mummy,
So to cheer him up, I gave him a pie.

Finally he found her
She stretched for twenty miles.
He screamed because he'd missed her
And now he always smiles.

Daniel Quinn (8)
Corpus Christi RC Primary School

UNTITLED

My friends at my school
Are really cool.

Rebecca,
Likes to play with Mica.

James,
Always ready for games.

Shelley,
Who loves to eat jelly.

Robyn,
Is always jogging.

Oliver,
Does not eat cauliflower.

Mason,
And his cousin Jason.

Joe,
Who is good at play dough.

And there is me
Gregory.

Greg Martin (9)
Corpus Christi RC Primary School

CZEBANNE

Her wings sparkle in the sea,
With a silver glint every time.
Her flippers move angelically,
Dashing glitter as she passes.
Her voice sounds oh so sweet,
Like a golden string of music twanging.
Her eyes glimmer in the moonlight,
Displaying jewels of beauty.
Her body is snow white,
With flowing stripes of silver down her back.
Her nose is pale pink,
Like a rose shining in the darkness.
Her tummy is full of spots,
Like diamonds shimmering in the sea.
Though I do not know what this creature is,
I still like to see its majestic appearance.

Hanna Thiel (10)
Corpus Christi RC Primary School

FRIENDS

You are my best friend,
We have a bond of pure metal
Nothing can bend.
Anything I need, you lend,
For you are my best friend,
All the colours of our lives blend,
You are my best friend!

Oliver Miccoli (9)
Corpus Christi RC Primary School

LADY

On Monday Lady robbed all the
Jewels
She's always breaking the human
Rules.
On Tuesday Lady went from roof to
Roof.
She went on the chimney pot and it just went
Poof!
On Wednesday she robbed Lloyds
Bank.
She left all her clues and fingerprints
Blank.
On Thursday Lady played a game of
Cards.
She got caught cheating and got kicked ten
Yards!
On Friday it was Lady's day
Off.
And she ended up with a pretty bad
Cough.
On Saturday she found out she had the
Flu.
And when she felt sick her face went
Blue!
On Sunday Lady started to
Cry.
Next minute she was starting to
Die.

Anna Gaw (10)
Corpus Christi RC Primary School

THE AGENT

Secret agent creeping around
Spies the enemy
Nearer and nearer, his heart begins to pound.

Takes out of his pocket a shiny black gun
For this professional
It seems just like fun.

Points the index and forefinger
Pulls back the thumb,
'Watch out Mister, here I come!'

Secret agent takes careful aim
'Oh! There goes the bell
The end of the game!'

Callum MacDermott (8)
Corpus Christi RC Primary School

BOYS AND GIRLS

Boys hate girls
Girls love boys
Or could it be
The other way round?
I wonder . . .
Like I do think
So boys are stupid
Girls are clever
As they say
Boys find chums
To have more fun
But girls go to college
To get more knowledge.

Yasmin Britton (8)
Corpus Christi RC Primary School

MY POEM

I love to go to football
To watch my favourite team
And when they score lots of goals
I scream and scream and scream
When they lose I get very sad
And shout 'Referee, you're mad!'

When the match is over
Off to home we go
Sometimes walking fast
Sometimes walking slow.

It's nice to get back in the warm
To see my mum and dad
I'll tell them all about the match
And what a great day I've had.

Hannah Dawson (9)
Corpus Christi RC Primary School

MONKEY

Monkey, monkey, having a laugh,
Monkey, monkey, splashing in the bath,
Monkey, monkey, swinging in the tree,
Monkey, monkey, got stung by a bee,
Monkey, monkey, driving a car,
Monkey, monkey, got lost in a jar
Monkey, monkey, went to the zoo,
Monkey, monkey, shouted 'Boo hoo',
Monkey, monkey, scratching his head
Monkey, monkey, went to bed.

Lucy Musgrave (9)
Corpus Christi RC Primary School

FINN'S WHEELS

When I'm on my blades I go really, really fast
Faster than a cheetah running through the grass.

Then I'm on my bike trying to do some tricks
Like hopping and wheeling and double whammy flips.

Then I'm on my skateboard trying to do a grind
Gonna get the trick right for my piece of mind.

Out on my surfboard gonna catch a wave
Waving to my mates yeah, Clayton, James and Dave.

Out having fun is really, really easy
Though I'd rather be at home doing what I pleasey.

Finn Donnelly (8)
Corpus Christi RC Primary School

MUM'S CRUSH

Mum drives me mad
She's got a big crush
It's really quite sad
She thinks Robbie's lush.

She dreams of Robbie Williams
I wish she'll concentrate
If he's on TV it's Robbie Williams
I dream that she'll be put straight.

She's got the CDs, the calendar and the books,
It's a frightful sight
She thinks he's got good looks,
Good looks, yeah right!

Alexandra Fellowes (10)
Corpus Christi RC Primary School

TEN NAUGHTY SCHOOL BOYS

Ten naughty school boys all messing about
One climbed over the fence and one began to shout.

That leaves eight naughty school boys by my calculations
One was late for class and one ruined the congratulations.

That leaves six naughty school boys left on their own
One set the fire alarm off and one used the school phone.

That leaves four naughty school boys being naughtier by the minute
One is rude to the head and one begins to fidget.

That leaves two naughty school boys looking for trouble
One knotted all the skipping ropes and the other tied them double.

That leaves no naughty school boys looking for attention
The headmaster caught them all and gave them a detention!

James Ethell (9)
Corpus Christi RC Primary School

WINTER SCENE

The snow lay heavy on the ground
Making it almost impossible to move
The tracks of the cars lay
Hidden under the snow.

The trees stood tall above
The bare bushes, icicles hang
Like monkeys from the thick heavy branches.

The boat was locked still on the frozen lake
So still it seemed like a frozen monster.

Samuel Goodman (10)
Corpus Christi RC Primary School

A GOOD JOB

When I am grown up I would like to be a builder -
Just like my dad.
He fixes things and makes people happy
Which makes him very glad.

He carries his tools in his van and a ladder on top
And drives to different jobs every day.
He works really hard and does not stop
All day but he enjoys his work anyway.

I've helped him move some bricks and dirt
He once even let me drive a digger.
It was great fun but my muscles hurt,
But when I got home they were definitely bigger!

Ryan Chancellor (8)
Corpus Christi RC Primary School

MY FAMILY

My little brother always wants to play
When I go to the park he always has to stay
My big brother hurts me when he's bored
And then he starts laughing.
Now it's my break call
My dad is very kind
Except when he is mad!
My mum is very kind
She helped me with my homework
That's the life I like.

Andrew Clarke (8)
Corpus Christi RC Primary School

THE SHUTTLE

Blasting off the ground,
Blasting off the floor,
Blasting into space,
Past the stars,
Went the shuttle.

Getting darker,
Darker still,
Running out of fuel
Suddenly
The pilot slipped onto the lever,
The lever snapped,
The engine ran out of fuel and shut down.

He pushed the bit of the lever
That wasn't snapped,
The engines started,
And they were speeding for planet Earth.
Home again.

Shane Cole (10)
Corpus Christi RC Primary School

THE NAUGHTY MONKEY

The naughty monkey jumped in the farm
He wanted to do some harm.
The naughty monkey bit the poor old donkey
Then he said 'My arm!'
He kicked the monkey in the straw.
The naughty monkey ran for his life,
For the donkey had a knife.

Maria-Helena Farah (7)
Corpus Christi RC Primary School

SNOWY DAY

White and fluffy on the ground.
Frost still falling on me,
Twirling round and round,
Granny calls me in for a nice cup of tea.

Watching it falling on the shed,
The cats jumping around,
All the flowers are now dead,
Bending down to the ground.

Put on my hat,
Then my coat,
Snow falling like a fluttering bat,
I'll pretend I'm sailing on a boat.

The sun's come out,
It's so hot,
No snow about,
It's melted the whole lot.

Stephanie Hayden (10)
Corpus Christi RC Primary School

STACEY AND LACEY

Stacey and Lacey
Slept in a shell.
Sleep little girls
You sleep so well.

Sleep little ladies,
Wake not soon!
The moon as your lamp
Glooming in your room.

Two bright stars
Peeped into the shell
Sounds of the dolphins
Dancing about.

Jade Gardener (9)
Corpus Christi RC Primary School

FLAMES

The roaring flames
Burning bright,
Spits and chokes,
Splutters and coughs.

Crackle, snap, bang,
Goes the fire,
The blazing fire
Roared and thundered.

Changing from colour to colour
Orange to yellow,
Blue, green, red then orange
Goldish yellow and purple too.

Its flames grow,
Bigger and bigger,
Fiercer and fiercer and
Brighter and brighter.

Its warm heat gets
Hotter and warmer,
Suddenly the fire dies down,
And it starts all over again.

Hannah Coope (10)
Corpus Christi RC Primary School

WINTER

It was a windy night,
As leaves fluttered
In the dark moonlit sky,
The waves crashed down
On the silky sand,
The trees sway like shimmering lace.

It's started snowing
Glittering snowflakes fall like butterflies
The snow shined as it fell to the ground,
The snow glides as the wind sweeps it up.

Crackling hailstones fall on the tops of people's houses
Crackle, crackle, crackle
Bang! Goes the thunder like a roaring lion.

Francesca McGrath (9)
Corpus Christi RC Primary School

THE WELLINGTON BOOTS

The wellington boots are dusty like my teddy bear Rusty.
When I get a new pair of wellington boots I want old rusty bear on them
But I'll tell you one thing that I don't want
I don't want them dusty.
Oh wellingtons has anybody bought you?
If they have I will scream and cry
And I'll have to say goodbye
Are we nearly there?
Yeah! There they are.
I'm pleased!

Yasmin Dow (8)
Corpus Christi RC Primary School

THE WORKER CROCODILE

Mr Crocodile had a day's work and said
'I am tired! I need a rest!
I can't work when I am tired
Cannot do my best'
He sighed and lay in the sand
His feet and his hand
Had sun shining down on them
As the moon came up.

His warm scaly body
Flamed like daisies and yellow gentle buttercups
Falling on the green crispy grass
His teeth as white and shining with light
As sharp as razors
As dangerous as lasers
The sun comes up
As he wakes.

Louis Higgins (9)
Corpus Christi RC Primary School

A FAT CAT THAT SITS ON A MAT

I have a fat cat that sits on a mat and he lies on it all day
But when I call him he comes for
His lunch but not for bedtime.
The dog came barking in
They jumped round all night but they get on all right,
Then in the morning I have to clear up
I had a cup of tea then
He spills it all over the kiwi.

William Simpson (8)
Corpus Christi RC Primary School

FOOD AT A PARTY

Food is gorgeous,
Food is great,
Food is the best thing at a party.

All of the chocolate
All to be ate
Chocolate is scrummy
Chocolate is sometimes runny.

Food is gorgeous,
Food is great,
Food is the best thing at a party.

All of the cake
And one more to make
Cake is fluffy,
Cake is never scruffy.

Food is gorgeous,
Food is great,
Food is the best thing at a party.

All bits of the biscuit
All to be gone
Biscuits are scrummy
And always crunchy.

Joshua Hayes (11)
Corpus Christi RC Primary School

MY PET BIRD

One day I saw a bird
There were a lot of them
My bird ate a berry and a cherry.

Charlotte Smith (8)
Corpus Christi RC Primary School

MY CHOCOLATE WORLD

Chocolate you are so yummy!
With your milky flavour,
You have that unique taste,
Everybody adores you.

My tummy goes haywire,
When I eat you
My nose goes bonkers,
When I smell you.

There are so many different
Types of chocolate
I don't know which to choose,
Dark or white you are all so nice.

You always give me energy
To do what I want
You never fail to make
Me happy.

Chocolate the nicest
Food in the world.

You are the best!

Michael Gibbons (10)
Corpus Christi RC Primary School

MY BIG BROTHER

My big brother's always driving me crazy
He makes my head spin
He says the grass is blue
And the sky is green.

Joseph Shean (8)
Corpus Christi RC Primary School

LISA THE GINGER CAT

Lisa went to the shop
To buy a mop
She cleaned the floor
And under the door.
She liked chips
And ate them with her fingertips
Her big, big dog
Can balance on a log.
There was a girl called Kelly
Her best friend was Shelly
Lisa had some money
And bought some honey.
Lisa had a nice day
On a sunny Sunday
She was sweet as a daisy
But very, very crazy.
Lisa was in a sub
And saw a cub.

Roisin Butler (7)
Corpus Christi RC Primary School

CATS

I have a Siamese cat
Who sits on a mat all day
I must admit he's rather skinny
Anyway he is a Siamese cat.
He's as white as snow
My little Siamese cat.

Dale Main (7)
Corpus Christi RC Primary School

THE TALE OF THE UNLUCKY TEN

Ten men running in a race,
One stopped to do his lace!
Nine men climbing up a wall,
One fell off and landed in a school!
Eight men skiing down a slope,
One got tangled in a rope!
Seven men rolling down a hill,
One got cold and caught a chill!
Six men running on a boat,
One of them found a mysterious note!
Five men out driving cars,
One drove into some tar!
Four men working with a tool,
One slipped on oil and fell in the pool!
Three men on a trip to a farm,
One got hurt serious harm!
Two men swimming in the sea,
One climbed out for his tea!
One man sitting on a bench,
Then it rained and he got drenched!

Christopher Clarke (10)
Corpus Christi RC Primary School

MY TWO SISTERS

I've got a sister she drives me mad
Sometimes she's happy, sometimes she's sad
My other sister she's really clever
She plays with my toys but I say never
Her name is Lenya the other's called Megan
I call them Benya and Silly Benya.

Aidan Rogers (8)
Corpus Christi RC Primary School

THE MOON

The moon shining bright,
Through the cold winter nights.
Twinkling stars,
Shining like Mars.
Shooting stars, zooming across the sky,
Like saying bye bye.
The clouds cover the moon,
But it's coming back soon.
The sun is coming up brightly.
The moon is going down lightly.
The moon is going to come up again.
I will look through my window about ten.

Sarah Coleman (9)
Corpus Christi RC Primary School

MY SISTER

My sister is cute,
My sister is kind,
She follows me always
Wherever I go.
My sister is funny.
She laughs at me too
But is this all true?
Yes.

My sister is funny
My sister is sweet
She makes a noise
When she sucks out of her teats.

Martha Nolan (8)
Corpus Christi RC Primary School

I HATE CHRISTMAS

I hate Christmas,
I never get what I've asked for
I think my mum and dad can't afford it
Because I think they're poor.

The reason they can't afford it
Is because it is too much.
All I want is a brand new bike,
Or a machine that makes
Chocolate sundaes
And the topping will be
Fudge.

Maybe a cheep BB Gun
Or a laptop PC
It's not fair!
My brother's got them,
They never think of me!

Sean Nunan (10)
Corpus Christi RC Primary School

THE GIRAFFE

I met a giraffe
Who wears a blue scarf
Who has brown spots
Oh he likes to eat pots
It makes me cross
But I call him Ross.

Cordelia Wilson-Read (7)
Corpus Christi RC Primary School

UNEARTHLY SHEEP

Sheep!
You think they're dumb
Sheep!
They're just having fun
Playing with your minds,
Oh!
Unearthly sheep!

New bulletin!
Computers found in barns,
Could this be the world of
Unearthly sheep?

They're from another world
A world of
Sheep!
They were sent as probes,
But didn't finish their mission,
And are,
Enjoying the lush green land!
Yes!
Enjoying the lush green land!

The bad thing is
Well for them
They cannot return,
Oh dear!
Oh dear!
Oh dear!

Good for us
Is that so
For the wool they bring.

If you listen carefully
You can hear them sing,
In the night that is,
Yes!
Unearthly sheep!

You see they're just like humans.

Robert Cassell (10)
Corpus Christi RC Primary School

MY POEM

Down behind the dustbin
I met a guy called Fred
I saw he didn't look too well
So I put him to bed.

Down behind the dustbin
I met a dog called Sam
He looked very hungry
So I gave him some ham.

Down behind the dustbin
I met a girl called Shelley
She looked quite normal
Until I saw her belly.

Down behind the dustbin
I met an elf called Neil
When I told my friends
They said elves aren't real.

Rachael Grierson (9)
Corpus Christi RC Primary School

D IS FOR DOLPHIN

D is for dolphins
    That I always think about.

O is for orange
    The colour of the sun.

L is for the low sun
    Which dolphins jump over.

P is for people
    Who ride on the boats.

H is for houses
    Where dolphins do not live.

I is for islands
    Which dolphins circle round.

N is for night sky
    Which dolphins like to look at.

S is for seaweed
    Which fish weave in and out of.

Michelle Sherwood (9)
Corpus Christi RC Primary School

I HATE PAINT

I hate paint
It makes me faint
It's all icky,
And it's all sticky
I hate paint.

Alexandra Burns (8)
Corpus Christi RC Primary School

MY CAT

My cat is fat
He eats twenty bags of rats a day
I tell him to pay
But he argues with me.

On Monday he eats thirty ice cream sundaes
He loves Mondays.

On Tuesday he sat on a bat
On my nice new mat.

On Wednesday he caught a bat
And I patted him on the back.

On Thursday he went to the gym
And did exercise to make him thin.

On Friday he went to the park
And jogged around until it got dark.

Alexandra Howarth (10)
Corpus Christi RC Primary School

I HAD A DREAM

I had a dream
I went in the deep blue sea
I saw three dolphins and they swam with me.
I swam deep on the ocean bed
With the three dolphins near my head
I felt the best
Now it was time to say goodbye
I felt very sad but I didn't cry.
Goodbye.

Camillantonia Mazzeo (9)
Corpus Christi RC Primary School

MY BABY SISTER

My baby sister is called Sorcha
She always runs around the house
She loves my grandad's cat Portia
Sometimes she creeps like a mouse.

She loves to play with her cousin Ollie
Although they sometimes fight
She occasionally calls him Lolly
They are together till Sunday night.

Her favourite colour is pink
She wears it all the time
She's nearly learnt to wink
And sing her nursery rhymes.

My baby sister loves our mum
She cuddles her all the time
My baby sister loves her mum
She likes to drink some lime.

Natacha Lockyer (10)
Corpus Christi RC Primary School

MY ROOM!

My room is nice and neat
The colours are hard to beat
The carpets are nice and green
I use a Hoover to keep them clean
The walls are painted blue and yellow
When I sit in here I feel mellow
My mum makes me keep it clean
I think she is very mean!

Peter Mallon (8)
Corpus Christi RC Primary School

THE DECISION

Light years away,
An alien has something to say
We shall invade Earth
The minute my mother gives birth.

We shall name the baby War,
But the alien stopped for what he saw
It appeared from space,
You should have seen the alien's face.

The creature was just a face,
But filled with his smiling case
I come from Earth
As his face filled with even more mirth.

Please don't harm my planet,
We have life forms such as Janet!
All the alien could do was nod
The creature said 'For I am God'.

Oliver Biles (10)
Corpus Christi RC Primary School

MY HAMSTER MONTY

My hamster Monty is very, very funny
He eats like a rabbit in a field
He builds his own home with paper and sawdust
And he drinks like a baby in a cot
He eats all his fruit that I give him
So he's a good little hamster after all
He loves to play with all kinds of people
Especially me and my mum.

Naomi Ellis (10)
Corpus Christi RC Primary School

MY TERRIBLE FAMILY

My horrible sister,
My idiotic brother.
My mess of a father,
My dreadful mother.

I've got a cool hamster,
His name is Boom.
Where does he live?
Well of course in my room.

My horrible sister,
She plays the flute.
What an awful racket,
That goes toot, toot, toot.

My idiotic brother,
Likes to punch and fight.
What time does he sleep?
Never at night.

My mess of a father
Crashed into the wall.
How did he do it?
He's just too tall.

My dreadful mother,
Has a pet dog.
Where did we get him?
Out in the fog.

Pippa Heath (8)
Corpus Christi RC Primary School

MY PET DOG

I have a dog called Wilf
He is huge and hairy
A bit like myself.

He likes to chase cats,
While they're lying peacefully on their mats.
The cats are fat and lazy
And think Wilf is a bit crazy.

People are scared,
When they knock on the door,
Wilf growls and barks,
But does no more.

When they see him,
They run with some pace,
But all he wants to do,
Is lick their face.

He likes to play,
But not all day.
You can hear him snore,
Form where he lay.
If he breaks anything,
He will pay.
Because he is clumsy
He just may.

He goes in the garden,
He makes a mess.
He causes my mum and dad,
Loads of stress.
But I don't care because I love him!

__Josh Sherriff (11)__
__Corpus Christi RC Primary School__

WHAT'S AFRAID?

Cats have whiskers,
Cats have hair
Cats have legs,
Four, four, four little legs.
Cats have claws,
Sometimes sharp
Cats are afraid of dogs
They are.

Dogs are hairy,
Dogs are big,
Dogs are small,
Dogs are vicious,
Dogs are cute,
Dogs are afraid of lions
They are.

Lions are hairy,
Lions have claws,
As sharp as a cat
Lions attack,
Lions roar!
Lions are afraid of bears
They are.

Bears are big,
Bears growl,
Bears are afraid of no one.

James Winyard (9)
Corpus Christi RC Primary School

MY FRIEND LUCY

Lucy is my friend's name
She is a girl of nine,
Being naughty is her game
It is her way of life.

She doesn't listen to her dad
Nor to her mother
Even if they get mad
She does not bother.

They tell her to do this
They tell her to do that
But she just gets in a mess
Because she's a little brat.

In school she doesn't do her work
She doesn't play with her friends
She always loves to talk and talk
The rules she always bends.

When she gets back to her home
She plays with her toys.
She interrupts on the phone
Oh, I wish she was good again.

Her favourite food is cheese
Her worst food is peas
When she gets ready for bed
She tries to stand on her head.

Madelon van Eerde (10)
Corpus Christi RC Primary School

NOISE

Guess who makes a lot of noise? Yes boys,
And are always messing around,
When I look at them they are always in style,
And when they see me I just look and smile.

Guess who makes a lot of noise? Yes boys,
Last night I saw them in the park,
They don't swing on the swings,
They just talk in the dark.

When those boys are making a noise,
I always wonder if they are allowed,
Because I have never seen one of their parents
Them boys have always been a big crowd.

I don't like those boys making a noise,
Because I don't like boys they pull girl's hair
And they spray silly spray all over flowers,
And that means they just don't care.

Sarah Barritt (10)
Corpus Christi RC Primary School

MY IMAGINATION

My imagination drives me mad,
And makes me fall asleep in the middle of class,
It really annoys my dad,
When I imagine things in Mass.

Sometimes I try not to imagine,
But I always do and it makes me go crazy,
I imagined once I was a dolphin,
But my mum woke me up and showed me a daisy.

The only problem is
I can't imagine when I want to go to sleep,
And it feels like years
Before I get to sleep.

Sam Satchwell (10)
Corpus Christi RC Primary School

PETS

P is for parrot that sits on a perch
   It copies what you say
   And stores it away
   Parrots always fly around
   Up, up, up and down
   They're very colourful but not that kind
   Nipping your fingers all the time.

E is for elephant with big stompy feet
   Walking around in the hot summer's heat
   Elephants squirt water from their big fat trunks
   Getting you soaking and making you get humps.

T is for tarantula with eight hairy legs
   Tickling your hands and
   Laying its eggs
   Running very quickly and making you scream
   Dropping from the ceiling and falling into your cream.

S is for snake long and thin
   Squirming about in the hot blazing sun
   Looking around for some fun
   Rolling and twisting but got shot with a gun.

Hayley Kennedy (9)
Corpus Christi RC Primary School

I WAS AT THE PARK

I was at the park
Going down the slide at night.
When suddenly a cat walked past,
I was as scared as a mouse.

I ran to the swings,
And I started to swing
When the cat walked past again,
I was as scared as a mouse.

I walked slowly to the roundabout
And started going round
When a dog walked past
I was as scared as a cat.

I skipped to the monkey bars
And started climbing
When another dog walked past
I was as scared as a cat.

It all went quiet,
The cat and the dog were gone.
I went back home
And the cat and the dog were mine.

Samantha Richardson (10)
Corpus Christi RC Primary School

HENRY

I have a rabbit called Henry
We thought he was born in February
He ate a lot of cherries
At Christmas he was merry.

They told us he was a mini lop
At Christmas he looked like five ends of a mop
They told us he was born in August
We didn't know but his cage was filled with sawdust!

Kourosh Tehrani (9)
Corpus Christi RC Primary School

MY PERSIAN CAT

I have a fluffy Persian cat
Who spends his days on a mat,
I must admit he's rather fat,
My fluffy Persian cat.

If a mouse would scuttle by
My cat would give a tired sigh.
He sees no point in chasing mice
He doesn't exactly find them nice.

My cat has many bell-shaped toys,
It's a pity they don't make a noise.
He never does any exercise
He says he does but they're just lies.

My cat is all pure white
He's never got in a fight,
He's always been as good as gold
And is the opposite of bold.

I like my cat though I complain,
Sometimes he drives me insane!
We have to treat him like a king
Next, he'll try to make us sing.

Shannon Main (10)
Corpus Christi RC Primary School

IN THE CLASSROOM

In the classroom
We work all day
And in-between
We play and obey.

In the classroom
We work all day
And at the end of each day
We pray.

In the classroom
We're not allowed to play,
If we do then
We pay.

In the classroom
We row and shout
And get told to
Stand out.

Zoe Barber (10)
Corpus Christi RC Primary School

JOE

There was a guy named Joe,
Who lost his middle toe.
He lost it in the army
By the shot of Sgt Barmy.

Sgt Barmy was his mate,
He must learn not to hesitate,
While Joe struggled with his injury
Sgt Barmy watched TV.

Stephen Bunting (10)
Corpus Christi RC Primary School

MY MYSTERY PET

I don't want a cat
Who eats fish and gets fat.

Or a monkey
Who acts all funky.

I don't want a fish
That Mum will eat as a Spanish dish.

Or a horse
That likes tomato sauce.

I don't want a snake
As thin as a rake.

I know what I want, I really do
What's his name?
I've forgotten too.

Sally Thom (10)
Corpus Christi RC Primary School

MY FLUFFY BUNNY

My fluffy bunny is very funny
She likes some honey on her toast
Sometimes she sees a ghost
That's when she boasts.

She saw a scary plate
She went to the lake
To bake a cake
She went for a swim
And saw her friend Kim.

Pierangela Marino (9)
Corpus Christi RC Primary School

A VARIETY OF ANIMALS

As stormy as a lion,
As meek as a mouse,
Some giraffes
Are as tall as a house.

As quick as a cheetah
As slow as a tortoise
As thin as a deer,
As fat as a porpoise.

The rabbits nibble
The hares run,
The mole keeps digging
But it's not for fun!

The cuckoos steal,
The geese squawk
The eagle soars,
The poor old ostrich can only walk!

From high in the mountains,
To deep in the sea,
All the animals live, happily.

Daniel Price (11)
Corpus Christi RC Primary School

THE SEASONS

In winter it is crisp and cold,
In spring it all begins to grow,
In summer it is very hot and sticky,
In autumn the leaves are all over the ground
And it's nice to play around.

Daniel Vigar (9)
Corpus Christi RC Primary School

THE WORLD TO COME

Just imagine the world to come
Full with robots and flying cars
And men could have babies out of their tum
And men and women flying to Mars.

Think of ray guns that put you to death
Think of new gadgets in your house
Think of rich people with even more wealth
Think of the amount of fleas in a robot mouse.

What if the sun doesn't shine?
What if there was no order and law?
What if the world was just a straight line?
What if there is always war?

Suppose children didn't go to school?
Suppose there would be no pets?
Suppose there was nothing called a pool?
Suppose that was as good as it gets?

Just say we couldn't eat
Just say we couldn't move
Just say vegetables were meat
Just say we could never approve.

This is not how I want it to be
Where not everyone has peace, just some
This is not the world I want to see
This is not the world I want to come.

Nicholas Waylett (11)
Corpus Christi RC Primary School

Frank

There once was a man called Frank
Who worked as a clerk in a bank
He thought it was funny
To nick all the money
And say it was all a prank.

Frank had a nasty boss,
His name was Larry Ross
He didn't think it funny
To nick all the money
And got really rather cross.

Sean Van Buiten (9)
Corpus Christi RC Primary School

The Dashing Frog

The frog who dashes through the streets
His eyes so bright filled with might
He makes his enemies feel so weak
He is called Nick the Mick.

Top of the frogs is Nick the Mick
Dashing past you, zooming towards you
Guess who it is? Nick the Mick!
He is here! He is there! He is everywhere!
That frog who dashes through the streets.

Salvador McCracken (9)
Corpus Christi RC Primary School

SEASONS

Winter is the season
Where kids play for a reason.

Summer is bright and light,
Summer is fun
Make sure you fly your kite.

Spring with flowers white and blue,
You will see the sheep maybe one or two.

Autumn is the time
When people collect the fruit and wine!

Emily Wentworth (8)
Corpus Christi RC Primary School

MY FAMILY

My dog Daisy
Is so crazy
And a bit mad
She's sometimes sad.

My sister Lizzy
Is so busy
She likes to go to the shops
To buy lots of tops.

My sister Jenny
She found a penny
She dropped it down a drain
In the biggest lane.

Jacquetta Bowley (9)
Corpus Christi RC Primary School

BOB

I know a man called Bob
He's got a very important job
He works all day
But he gets very good pay
He's got a big flash car
And he likes to drive it far and far and far.

Christy O'Grady (8)
Corpus Christi RC Primary School

SPRINGTIME

The days are getting warmer,
The birds are beginning to sing
I think they are trying to tell us
That it will soon be spring.

The days are getting longer,
The buds are starting to sprout,
And down in the pond in my garden
The frogs are moving about.

It won't be long until springtime
The trees and flowers will grow
The animals will come out of hibernation
How do they seem to know?

Now that springtime's here at last
I'm sure you will agree,
There are lots of new and wondrous things
For everyone to see.

Ryan Johnson (10)
Heathlands Primary School

MY NEW SPORTS CAR

My new sports car goes very fast
I keep on thinking of the past
Where my old car used to be
Locked away with the key.

But now I have my new sports car
I take it everywhere I go really far
Now I can go really fast
Now I don't remember the past.

I can't believe I go as fast as lightning
It even gets people fighting
The patrol is made of fire
It even goes through metal wire.

I have no job
My name is Rob
I hate using knives
But I have a lovely wife.

My sports car is the best
I take it for a drive but then he has a rest
I love it so much
It has a special touch.

I'm glad I got my lovely car
I ride it everywhere it takes me far
It rides so fast
Now I never remember the past.

My past is with my new car
All the times when we drove fast
My car's the best
It's my sports car!

Melissa Mitchell (9)
Heathlands Primary School

THE STORM

One night it was dark
And you could hear dogs bark.
The wind was blowing
The sky kept glowing.

The floor rumbled
And then it grumbled
There was lightning
Then again thundering.

The storm stopped
And something popped
There was a hole in the ground
Nobody made a sound.

Laura Ellis (9)
Heathlands Primary School

SPIDERS

Some spiders have long legs,
Some spiders have short legs,
Some spiders like bathrooms,
But most of the time they drown.
Spiders are so creepy,
I do not know about you
Spiders have eight legs
And we only have two
Some are big, some are small
I don't know about you but I hate spiders
Spiders are so friendly they would not hurt a fly.

Joey Croft (11)
Heathlands Primary School

HONEY AND HER PUPS

Honey came from Wales
And was so sad
As some people there
Treat her bad.

She came to our house
Which is nice and warm
Where she had two pups
Called Phats and Small.

Honey is so funny
Her pups are too!
Honey and her pups
We love you!

Gemma Dean (8)
Heathlands Primary School

MY NAN

People are old
Sitting in a chair
Eating Weetabix,
Always stares,
She never tries to exercise
But all she ever does is sit in her chair
Drinking her cups of tea
Getting mad
She goes to hit me but she
Always falls back down again
She has a stick but never uses it
She has to be looked after by daughters.

Marc Harris (8)
Heathlands Primary School

WHAT IS A COLOUR?

What is pink?
A pig is pink, rolling in a stink.

What is red?
Poppies are red, in the flower bed.

What is blue?
You are blue, when you have the flu.

What is white?
A wedding dress is white, like snow crispy and bright.

What is yellow?
The sun is yellow, being a good fellow.

What is green?
A runner bean is green, sitting on a hat so mean.

What is black?
A cat is black, sitting on a doormat.

What is grey?
The sky is grey, on a stormy day.

Sophie Harding (8)
Heathlands Primary School

THE SEA

The sea is like a ferocious bear in pain.

The sea is like a beautiful Persian cat chasing a rat.

The sea is like a fluffy lion chasing its prey.

The sea is like a calm sleeping cat.

Craig Biddle (9)
Heathlands Primary School

WHAT IS GOLD?

What is gold?
The sun is a big ball of gold
Shining on the young and old!

What is green?
The grass is green
Beautiful and clean lucky no glass there to stand on.

What is red?
A strawberry is red
Waiting to be fed, waiting in its bed.

What is pink?
A rose is pink
Sparkling in a beehive that cleans around the time being.

What is white?
A label is white,
A piece of white is white crying in a bed.

Abbie Legg (9)
Heathlands Primary School

MY CHEESY FEET

My cheesy feet they are so cheesy
They make me feel wheezy.

I love cheese but the taste it is out
Of this world, they will have to have paste.

Even aliens can't stand the smell
And they are out of this world
Because it makes them twirl.

Danyella Croucher (9)
Heathlands Primary School

DON'T DROP LITTER

Don't drop litter put it in the bin,
Don't drop litter put it in the bin,
So let's put our school to the test,
So don't drop litter put it in the bin.

Don't drop crisp packets put them in the bin,
Don't drop crisp packets put them in the bin,
So let's put our school to the test,
So don't drop crisp packets put them in the bin.

Don't drop cans put them in the bin,
Don't drop cans put them in the bin,
So let's put our school to the test,
So don't drop cans put them in the bin.

Don't drop bottles put them in the bin,
Don't drop bottles put them in the bin,
So let's put our school to the test,
So don't drop bottles put them in the bin.

Don't drop litter put it in the bin,
Don't drop litter put it in the bin,
So let's put our school to the test,
So don't drop litter put it in the bin.

Karen Whiting
Heathlands Primary School

ON HOLIDAY

I was on holiday
And it was hot
I was on holiday
And my dad bought a Greek pot
It was pink and blue, yellow too
And I caught the flu.

My mum got some frying pans
My aunty too,
I had a silver watch
That had a digital clock
The time came
To leave La
Nothing to say
Except see you La.

Kurt Barter (10)
Heathlands Primary School

MY WORST HOUSE

When I open the door and slam it shut
When the door handle falls off
When I go up the creaking stairs
With no carpet on them.

Spider webs in the corner of rooms
You can't sweep them cos there aren't any brooms
A bedroom with no TV
In the lounge it's too small for me.

When you go to the kitchen
You'll be going mad
It's a mess everywhere
It looks like it's a war.

When you make it to the bathroom
You're going to be shocked into doom
It's the only room that's clean
Finally I've found a good clean room.

Jason Coombs (10)
Heathlands Primary School

The Storm

The storm makes the great crash against the rocks,
The bright lightning that lights up the sky
The storm makes the big blue boats crash against the pathways
The storm scares children by tapping against their bedroom windows.

The storm that makes a big crash, wallop, bang,
The storm makes waves crash and go on the paths,
The storm is scary and makes me want to cry,
The storm goes like this shhhh . . .
It's stopped.

Chelsea Jones (10)
Heathlands Primary School

The Gazing Moon

The gazing moon shines in the gloom,
As it lights up the distant east.

The gazing moon shines so bright,
It leaves a golden trail.

With the barn owls hooting
As they glide through the velvet golden trail.

When the gazing moon comes out to play,
You're sure to see his smiley face
When he plays kiss chase, with the stars.

The gazing moon.

Stephanie Churchill (9)
Heathlands Primary School

I Wish

I wish I could fly to the broken clouds,
I wish I could sing to the open air,
I wish I could swim the ocean blue,
I wish I could dive with the dolphin's crew,
I wish I could run to my friends among the busy bends.

I want to hunt for blocks of gold which lie beyond the cave of Mold
I want to buy a dozen sweets 'cause they are my dream beliefs.

I wish I could ride my bike down the biggest hill in London,
I wish I could sing to the elderly to make them happy.
I wish my brother could grow out his of his nappies,
I wish I could climb up to the blazing sun.

Chloe Diamond (9)
Heathlands Primary School

My Dog

My dog is small, black and brown
He always used to be running around.
But now he is older he just
Watches telly on his belly.
Then goes to bed with his ted to
Dream about the next day ahead.

That's my dog
Mali
Woof, woof!

Tanya Brierley (11) & Samantha Waldron (10)
Heathlands Primary School

MY DOG AND ME

Mason, my dog is bigger then me
Because he's a St Bernard dog you see
I go with my dad to take him for walks
If I can't be bothered and don't want to talk
Then I stay indoors and watch TV
Because I like cartoons you see.

Lisa Fitzpatrick (11)
Heathlands Primary School

I LOVE MUPPEY AND MUPPEY LOVES ME

I love Muppey and Muppey loves me
We try to live in harmony
When it is a cold night
Muppey and me cuddle up tight
I love Muppey and Muppey loves me
We try to live in harmony.

Lauren Coat (8)
Heathlands Primary School

AN ELEGY

My life has been shattered in pieces,
My soul has been broken,
My laughter has turned to tears,
My world is upside down,
My music is gone,
No longer to live,
All that is lost,
Will never be the same.

Ryan Balch (9)
Kingsleigh Junior School

IN MY CLASS

In my class:

Chloe is a fresh, cool breeze,
She's a right goal winner,
She's a baby blue-bell,
And can be an angry bumblebee.

In my class:

Shaunna is a golden buttercup,
She's a juicy watermelon,
She's the sweetness in honey,
And a top gold medal.

In my class:

Lisa is a blazing sun,
She's the echo in the subway,
She's the powerful pink of a pig,
And a great big grin.

Stevie Wright (10)
Kingsleigh Junior School

OUR PLAYGROUND

Yippee! It's playtime!
Before we go out to play we all search for our fruit.
Let's go and have a glorious time.
Our voices echo in the tunnels on adventure.
While the teachers watch us play
We play with hand-tennis you know.
Everyone enjoys the water fountains.
When the bell goes the fun is over.
Now the playground is silent.

Lauren Fox (9)
Kingsleigh Junior School

LOVE IS WASTED

My love has gone, my life has ended.
The spirit of the one I need,
I shall not live this moment long.

The good in my life has faded.
The bad has come,
I need you back.

I'd risk my life to see thee again.
The day has come where it hurts,
Please come back I need you so.

Eurydice, Eurydice why us to part?
Memories still stand in my heart.

Daniel Ellis (10)
Kingsleigh Junior School

OUR PLAYGROUND

Before we go out we find our fruit,
We play lots of games,
There's loads of balls bouncing in netball.
Bang, bang, bang,
Goes the big hand-tennis,
But adventure is the best,
Let's hope we have enough nuggets
To have an extra adventure this week,
Children shouting in the playground,
Like noisy elephants.
When the bell goes the fun is over.
Then we work hard.

Rebecca Charig (9)
Kingsleigh Junior School

AND MY HEART SOARS

The scent of red roses.
The freshness of the air.
The taste of haddock.
Speak to me.

The iciness of icicles.
The darkness of the evening.
The horizon of the sunset.
Speak to me.

The twinkle of the stars.
The brightness of the moonlight.
The roughness of the sea.
Speak to me.

Charlotte Millett (9)
Kingsleigh Junior School

OUR PLAYGROUND

The children run out at playtime to freedom.
'It's our adventure!' people cry.
Running to adventure, as fast as a cheetah.
Last one to the skis.
There's not many there.
Let's go on the mound.
Watch out for stinging nettles.
We play It, tunnel's home.
Let's play draughts, four people to play.
Let's play with the big hand-tennis.
When the bell goes
Fun is over.

Jennifer Rizza (9)
Kingsleigh Junior School

AND MY HEART SOARS

The scent of the flowers,
The freshness of the morning dew,
The fragrance of the forest trees,
Speak to me.

The icy peak of the hills,
The fresh spring from the sky,
The crashing of the waves,
Speak to me.

The glow of the moon,
The pitch-black of the night,
The dew drop on the grass,
Speak to me.

The flesh of deer,
The flavour of fish,
The trail of cattle,
And the life that never goes away,
Speak to me.

And my heart soars.

Paul Kim (9)
Kingsleigh Junior School

AND MY HEART SOARS

The glistening of the sun.
The glow of the moonlight.
The twinkling of the stars.
Speak to me.

The rushing of the river.
The juices of the fruit.
The strength of the trees.
Speak to me.

The frost in the winter.
The darkness of the night.
The grazing of the deer.
Speak to me.

Hannah Moore (10)
Kingsleigh Junior School

IN MY FAMILY

In my family:

Dad is the crunch in the autumn leaves,
He is the winning goal in tennis,
He is a giant flower in a garden.
He is the swirling tornado in a storm.

In my family:

Mum is a daisy on a flower bed,
She is the eye in a tornado,
She is polish and a feather duster.

In my family:

My brother is a fly buzzing in your ear,
He is the floppy jelly,
He is the nightmare in a dream,
He is the burning in a fire.

In my family:

That leaves me
And I'm . . .
Not telling!

Marc Crook (10)
Kingsleigh Junior School

IN OUR FAMILY

In our family,
Rhiannon is a bowl of cereal,
She's a security guard,
She's a mucky pup
And she's a smelly pair of smelly trainers.

In our family,
Max my dog is a security dog,
He's a smelly towel,
He's a mucky pup
And he's thunder and lightning.

In our family,
BJ, my mum's bird, is a noisy motorbike,
He's a cuddly feather duster,
He's as still as a statue,
He's a bunch of grapes.

Martin Vivian (10)
Kingsleigh Junior School

OUR PLAYGROUND

Before we go out we search for our fruit,
All the shouting from out the door.
In the quiet area it is as quiet as a mouse,
In the playground it is as noisy as can be.
On the adventure we can hear voices echoing in the tunnels.
Some girls and some boys play netball trying to catch the ball.
As soon as the bell goes we stop,
Dead quiet!

Cassie Lazenbury (8)
Kingsleigh Junior School

IN MY CLASS

In my class:

Stevie is the colour in the flowers,
She is the beauty of a dolphin,
But she can be an angry goat.

In my class:

Shaunna is a swan,
She is a jack-in-the-box,
She is a tall pine tree.

In my class:

Chelsea is an elegant eagle swooping in the air,
She is a little cat,
She is as angry as a wasp.

Chloé Hooper (10)
Kingsleigh Junior School

THE WIND IS A HUNGRY WOLF

The wind is a hungry wolf,
Ready to attack.
It searches for its prey in the moonlight.
It rushes through the crunchy brown leaves.
Prowling in the forest.
Moving swiftly in the wilderness.
Howling at the moon.
The wind is calm.
The wolf settles in its cave.

Adam Higgins (10)
Kingsleigh Junior School

AND MY HEART SOARS

The aroma of the wild flowers,
The warmth of the bright sun,
The freshness of the cool water,
Speaks to me.

The juiciness of the berry,
The dew from the fresh green grass,
The bitterness of the wind,
Speak to me.

The moisture of the brown soil,
The sound of the swaying trees,
The power of the fierce bears,
Speak to me.

My heart soars.

Elizabeth Heron (10)
Kingsleigh Junior School

OUR PLAYGROUND

It's playtime,
Everybody makes a noise in the playground.
We love the water fountains.
The basketball in the playground.
Our new games of hand-tennis
Out of our new playground bags.
We find our juicy fruit.
In the quiet area it is as quiet as mice.
We play draughts on adventure.
When the bell goes
The fun is over.

Lee Bartaby (7)
Kingsleigh Junior School

IN MY CLASS

Tamzin is the spring flowers,
She is the friend of the universe,
She is the 'yes' I wish was a 'no'.

In my class:

Katie is the flash of a disco light,
She is a quick glance of the moon,
She is the taste of chocolate,
And she is the graceful snowflakes.

In my class:

Linda is the fresh air of a valley,
She is the look of a firework,
She is the fun of a fairground,
And she is the warmth of a sun.

Emily Hackin (10)
Kingsleigh Junior School

ORPHEUS' ELEGY

Everything was beautiful in the beginning,
Until you died you were my love.
You were my light, my world,
Nothing can replace you.
Oh why did you go to the place of fire?
No more will my tunes be sweet, but of death.
Eurydice was your name.
You were my life, also my sun.
You showed me love and light.
You were the star of my life,
You were my passion, my all.

Rosie Dimmer (9)
Kingsleigh Junior School

IN OUR FAMILY

Dad's the twist in a roller coaster,
He's the sofa in our living room,
He's the light in a dark night,
He's a tornado destroying anything in his path.

In our family:

Mum's the cleanliness of the new shower,
She's the sunburn from the beach,
She is a rose ready to prick,
She's the new sun each day.

In our family:

James is the constantly talking TV,
He's as cute as a kitten,
He's the bite from a dog,
He's the cuddle in a teddy.

In our family:

That leaves me!
And I'm . . . no
Not really!

Steven Sheehy (10)
Kingsleigh Junior School

CLOUDS

Blue and pink candyfloss twisting on a stick.
Vanilla and strawberry ice cream in a large blue bowl.
The black flock of sheep grazing in the pink and blue fields.
Bubbles floating in the silver bath.

Vivienne Henstridge (8)
Kingsleigh Junior School

HAPPY CAT

I am a cat curled up on a rug,
Feeling really safe and snug.
It's really wet and cold outside,
So I'll stay indoors and try to hide.

When I'm awake I chase my ball,
Up and down the winding hall,
Feeling hungry I rub round feet,
Meowing for my favourite meat.

Time for play I hide to pounce,
Over the chairs I have to bounce,
Running round and round the room,
Whizzing up the curtains – zoom!

Really tired, time to sleep,
Next to the fire in a big heap.

Rachel Innes (9)
King's Park Primary School

MOUNTAINS

High in the sky like a king.
Looking down, never do I see people looking at me.
I dream of birds coming for a drink in my springs,
Or people coming to take a look at the indescribable feeling.
Natural plants with natural air.
Icy at the top and a peaceful atmosphere bare.
All ready for lots of rocks to disappear.
Crumbly and raggy you will see if you come and look at me.
Mysterious and breathtaking I am to see.
I would love to see mountains bigger than me.

Molly McCann (10)
King's Park Primary School

My Computer

Our new computer
Is very super
It does funny things
Makes little ticks and loud pings
There's loads of boxes
Big and small
But the CPU
Is not flat but tall.
There's miles of cables
Round the back
All going to plugs
Painted black.
When we eventually
Switched it on
It worked for a while
Then the modem went wrong.
Now it's fixed we surf the world
Visit places I've never heard.
Travel time, it's really super
I'm very pleased with my new computer.

Portia Criswick (10)
King's Park Primary School

The Ant And His Only Friend

One day I saw a little ant crawling on its own.
I took its hand, said hello and then walked it home.
I asked where his friend might be,
He said he didn't have none,
'Yes you do, you've got me,'
And I cuddled him under the sun.

Lisa Curtis (10)
King's Park Primary School

WARMTH

Warmth is my cosy bed,
The bright sun touching my head.

Warmth is the feeling I get,
When I stroke my pet.

Warmth is my best jumper,
And my cosy coat.

Warmth is a hot roast dinner,
The glowing coal in a fire.

Warmth is knowing when I cry,
My parents are there to ask me why.

Warmth is my cuddly bear,
Christmas pudding ready to share.

Amber Wood (9)
King's Park Primary School

THE RAINFOREST

Monkeys swinging through the trees,
Tigers prowling underneath,
Leopards dotted,
Cheetahs spotted,
Bright red frogs,
And water hogs,
Exotic birds,
To be heard,
Snakes and spiders,
Climbing higher,
Animals and plants filling all the space,
A beautiful rainforest is this amazing place.

Christina Bradley (10)
King's Park Primary School

MY FOUR DOGS

My favourite dog Charlie,
Is always asleep,
He sometimes awakes,
But that's just to eat.
He goes to the park for a walk in the car,
And he is so old he can't walk that far.

My other dog April,
Is as mad as can be,
She is also very old,
But very lively.
She runs round and round,
And goes with me to school,
She's really quite mad and acts like a fool.

My nanny's dog Mutley,
Looks like a big cuddly bear,
A big ball of fluff,
With far too much hair.

Her other dog Sheba,
Now she rules the house,
With a big fluffy tail,
And a head like a mouse.

Frances Fletcher (10)
King's Park Primary School

MOUNTAINS

A death trap to many people,
An element of fear.
Pointed edges digging into your skin,
The crumbling rocky formation.
Towering over the highest clouds,
Avalanches trapping people, never to be seen again.

The breathtaking scenery,
Natural and fresh,
Peaceful and stunning.
Mysterious in its own way.
In the sunset the mountains are orange,
Glowing in the sun.

Fizza Haider (11)
King's Park Primary School

GIRLS

Girls are fantastic,
Girls are cool,
Girls like to sunbathe
And swim in the pool.

Girls are always laughing,
They love to gossip and talk,
They're always up for a sleepover
But never a cross-country walk.

Girls like to talk about fashions,
They're always up to date,
Girls are so unlike boys
Because boys always get in a state!

Girls like to be naughty and cheeky,
They love to be loud and rude,
And another reason that they differ from boys
Is that they hardly ever get in a mood!

Girls don't like the cold winters,
They like to stay out in the sun,
And it's true what Cyndi Lauper said -
Girls just wanna have fun!

Tara Lonnen (10)
King's Park Primary School

MY DOG

My dog Sally is black as coal,
Her hazel eyes are like windows to her soul.
I wake in the morning to lots of kisses.
When I'm at school it's me she misses.

We go to the park and play ball.
Of my friends she's the best of all.
She's my best pal,
My dog Sal.

When I got her she was nine weeks old,
From a farm she was sold
In far away Devon,
She was a gift from Heaven.

Mathew Chilton (10)
King's Park Primary School

A MOUNTAIN

A mountain is a giant hill,
With emerald green forests,
It is extremely mysterious,
And it is very precious,
It is the king of nature,
Which has colourful splendour,
A mountain is where the sun rises
And where the sun sets,
At the top of the mountain is an angry monster,
Which hurts every visitor.
At the bottom of the mountain,
Is a gentle friend,
Which lets you have a peaceful time in its palace.

Sunghee Kim (10)
King's Park Primary School

GROWING UP

First off for girls it's dolls and such
And boys like football just as much.

Then you start to take these silly pictures off the wall
The ones that when your friends see you feel a fool.

Next it's off to secondary school, separated from your friends
You think the pain will never end.

Next it's out of school to get a job, to get a home,
Now you're in the adult zone.

Yes you've married you feel so wild,
Next thing you know you've got a child.

You're feeling ill you're feeling faint
Maybe it's something you ate.

Now your eyes begin to close
As you fall into an eternal doze.

Emily Easthope (10)
King's Park Primary School

MOUNTAINS

Like old feeble faces
All crumpled from years gone by
Whirlwinds causing havoc
And streaking its aged face
Sunrise to sunset the mountain is praised
Glistening up in the sky
Surrounded and shrouded with mist
Snow like whipped cream.

Anna Savage (11)
King's Park Primary School

The Storm

The storm is a villain plotting evil against you.
Its noise is the scream of a child.
The storm is a battle between Earth and wind.
The dark sky is its black, scheming eyes
Watching your every move.
Its breath is a hurricane spinning round and round.
Its hands reach out and pull you towards it.
Its gigantic feet stomp down trees and houses,
Aiming for you.
The storm cuts down the power
Hoping to scare everybody in town.
The storm's eye waters and floods the town.
The storm gets stronger and the screams get louder.
The storm is a powerful being, too strong for us to conquer.

Katy Dimech (11)
King's Park Primary School

Mountains

High, jagged, elevated rocks,
Snow like freezing cold ice cream,
It's like the end of a shiny, sharp knife.
Towering above the sky, they're so high,
Just like a glistening mirror
For someone to look in.
Tiny flowers under your clumpy boots,
Small pieces of rock crumbling off the top;
They will always be peering above
The clouds.

Elliot Fensom (10)
King's Park Primary School

MAGIC BOX

I will put in the box:
The glance of a genie when he grants you a gift,
A terrifying T-rex tumbling a toothless turtle.
A clumsy cat covered in creamy chocolate clusters.
A six-legged spineless spider scared by slimy snail tracks.
A cheeky chipmunk challenging a chimpanzee to chess and
The flap of a bird's wing on a winter's dawn.
My box is made from wood from the very deepest Caribbean oceans,
Its hinges are made from icicles from the sparkling Mount Everest
And its padlock has a live snake's head on
That glistens in a third dimension in a black sun.
I will roll in my box till I am covered with love and joy,
Happiness and comfort, and my face is dancing with glee.
Then I shall hide the box in the coldest, darkest place in the universe,
Never to be opened again.

Freya Coles (10)
King's Park Primary School

MOUNTAINS

The towering indented rocks pierce the sky,
Snow like whipped cream settles on the top.
As the whistling wind blows they become shrouded in mist,
It's a crumbling tower with ice like glistening teeth.
They are pointed ears on an ageing face,
They are the great watchers of the world
Looking out onto their kingdom.
Forever they will stand.
Alone.

Vanessa Miles (10)
King's Park Primary School

AMAZING COLOURS

Fiery, dangerous hot lava rocks hurl at you
Whilst the hot lava flows down destroying anything in its path.
Like a scaly dragon, ferocious, frightening, tall
Burning anything that attempts to kill it.

The rusty coloured sand dunes of the Arabian desert,
Burning brightly as it takes in the burning heat from the glowing sun.

The Amazon forest with shades of lush grass and leaves,
A mamba sliding through the trees silently, then bang it's
                                              caught its prey.
A shiny, sparkling emerald; the precious stone that reflects the light
                                              as rich colours of the trees

A sparkling, glittery sea, water ripples crashing against the rocks.
A sparkling, velvety dolphin leaps out of the waves against the dark
                                              gloomy night sky.
A beautiful night sky showing off the shiny, gold stars.
Crude oil slowly covering the water like a blanket over the sea.
Ominous looking like coal, threatening with dirt and dust.

Kristopher Hearsum (10)
St Mark's Primary School

UNDER MY FILTHY BED

When I looked under my filthy bed,
I saw a very dark gloomy sky,
But then a spaceship with lights hovering above.

When I looked under my bed
I saw a ballet dancer pirouetting under the stars and moon,
Then suddenly walking along a dark street,
A parade of ghosts from Victorian times.

When I looked under my filthy bed
I saw people in America playing drums round a fire.
I could see them just coming back from a hunt,
Hungry and ready to eat.

When I looked under my filthy bed,
I saw everything just as it was,
With all my toys spread around.

Jenny Houston (9)
St Mark's Primary School

COLOURS

Rippling fire spurting out of a dragon's red raw nose,
Squirming, scaly jellyfish dodging in and out of the whirling mist.
Lava in a lava lamp shining in the spotlight of a show.
A wobbly, wibbly, waiting jelly stuck in a boredom fantasy.

Seaweed drifting towards the shore,
Watching and waiting for the feet of a human.
Dancing leaves longing for a friend.
Swirling mist pushing people into an unknown world.
Moss perched on a rock, glued to the spot.

Tidal wave spitting water over the world like a water pistol.
The sky on a hot boiling day.
A waterfall trickling down into a pool of wonders.

A mouthful of candyfloss melting in the saliva of a sweet mouth.
A night sky which will bring blinding sun to follow.
Puff of a princess' perfumes,
Bringing a smell which is out of your mind.
Handfuls of bursting buds, ready to bloom with flowers.

Rebecca Brown (11)
St Mark's Primary School

COLOUR POEM

The dragon breathing hot burning flames
Burned everything in its way,
As people ran for their lives
As the dragon rampaging throws the target to its lair.

The long fresh green grass tickled
My scaly green toes
As I hopped onto a lily pad,
As though I was a toad.

The blue crashing waves
Of the deep blue ocean,
As a blue bottle-nosed dolphin
Jumped out of the crashing waves.

The hot burning sun blazed down
On the sizzling sandy desert.

Jonathan Wheatley (11)
St Mark's Primary School

COLOUR

A volcano, a huge volcano
Erupting molten lava,
A dead body being ripped to shreds,
A candle burning as bright as the sun,
A frog leaping through the air into misty green water.
Big, green fields, lush grass,
A green lizard under a damp rock.
Dolphins, a beautiful gentle dolphin
Swimming on the ocean bottom.
The big blue ocean sea
A deep blue sky which never ends.

Jacob Stanley (11)
St Mark's Primary School

COLOUR POEM

A jellyfish squirming in the light,
Crystal blue sea, as night begins,
Blood travelling in somebody's body.

Oil escaping from an oil tanker
And travelling around the petrol station,
Gems and jewels in jewellery.

A frog jumping and hopping
Around the green, green grass,
An old green pond with algae on it.

The sun boiling and blazing the sand on the beach.
But the sea still cold.
A torch shining in the cold dark night.

Luke Granger (10)
St Mark's Primary School

CATS CAN DO ANYTHING

Cats can kill with an instant bite,
They stalk their prey mostly at night,
They're silent stalkers that can swiftly kill
Or just leave the lifeless rats ill.

They can dance and prance and sing to the moon
Like the mermaids in the lagoon
They get chased by dogs run, run, run,
If they make it, they laugh and think it's fun.

Then they lie by the fire and have some rest,
Accompanied by their master, to whom they're never a pest.

Oliver Barton (11)
St Mark's Primary School

MY CAT

My cat is evil in a way,
Blackest fur she cleans all day.
Creeping slowly through the grass,
Pounces quickly, kills clean and fast.

Killing everything in sight,
Even every carpet mite.
Sharpening those pointy claws,
Hiding in black velvet paws.

Her tail's like a lashing whip,
If she's angry watch it flick.
Showing all her whitened teeth,
Even when she goes to sleep.

Her glowing green eyes reflect the light,
Even in the darkest night.
Any male that wants to kiss,
She will give her meanest hiss.

Carla Gosling (11)
St Mark's Primary School

COLOURS

The hot lava, bubbling
Non-stop exploding
Out of the hot volcano
Rumbling, tumbling into the sea.

The harmless seaweed
Floating gently, swiftly
Making its way
Slowly but surely to the shore.

The shiny, silky dolphin
Swiftly swims his way through
The calm waves of
The deep, deep sea.

The killer whale swims up
And down jumping and
Firing water through its
Shiny, rubbery, slimy wet back.

Samantha Reeves (11)
St Mark's Primary School

THE KILLER

The killer has clasping, clever claws,
Teething, tight, teeth,
And powerful, perfect paws.

As it creeps slowly and unwarily
Across the forest of grass
A mouse goes past the house
The killer lays ready to pounce.
Its brown fur camouflaged in the dirt,
Its green eyes a sapphire gleaming bright,
It pounces down, down, down.

Its paws laid out on the sun
Covered in blood from lunch
He has his tail swinging like an aerial
Searching for a bird to smother with its
Clever, clasping claws,
Terrifying, terrible teeth,
And powerful, perfect jaws.

James Crotty (11)
St Mark's Primary School

MY GINGER CAT

I have a ginger cat,
Who sits upon my lap,
When I stroke and pat,
The ginger cat,
That's sitting on my lap.

Its eyes are big and bold,
The cat is very old,
Its paws are small and fury,
Its ginger hair is curly.

I have a ginger cat,
Who sits upon my lap,
Where I stroke and pat,
The little cat,
That is sitting on my lap.

Sophie Phillips-Pitman (10)
St Mark's Primary School

CAT

The sleek, smooth predator.
Razor claws like a guillotine,
The deadly foe elongates its carving knives
And prepares to pounce on the unwary meal.

The calm cat advances on the mouse.
The silence is deafening.
The cat edges towards the prey,
The movement like a reflex action to the feline.
Then with split-second timing, he pounces,
The mouse is history.

Sam Cooper (11)
St Mark's Primary School

MARMALADE

Marmalade,
He spread out so sweet,
His paws were nice and taut,
But when he scratched me,
I got so mad,
We nearly went to court!

Marmalade,
He wasn't so nice,
He always kept so cool,
There was one time I do recall
He fell into the swimming pool.

Marmalade,
He wasn't young,
But he played with balls of twine,
He lived before we retire him,
To an ancient 39!

Marmalade,
He was so mean,
His claws were never blunt,
He played poker
With the other cats,
The dirty little runt!

Marmalade,
Now in this closing sentence,
I need another cat,
Preferably one,
Who isn't terribly
Rude or fat!

Matthew Gunter
St Mark's Primary School

GINGER THE CAT

Ginger eyes they glare with fright,
In the night they shine so bright.
His ears, they twitch in the air,
Listening for trouble to pounce and scare.

Ginger the cat strolls around,
His velvet paws upon the ground.
His claws, they are as sharp as knives,
To other cats they find him nice.

Ginger's little nose twitches up and down,
While he hits his ball on the ground.
His fur is thick and soft,
His favourite place is the loft.

He purrs while sitting by the fire,
When it comes to jumping off walls, he tends to be quite a flier,
His tail, it wiggles side to side,
While walking towards Mrs Glide.

Mrs Glide is a kind old lady,
Who leaves food out for Ginger and makes sure he has plenty.
Ginger's belly is full of food,
Now he needs to have a snooze.

Gemma Henry (10)
St Mark's Primary School

CAT

Wandering wearily
Along on its own,
Trudging, trailing,
In the dewy moist grass.
Pondering peacefully,
The cat is like a sleepy bat,
Careless cat.

Creeping carefully,
Snooping, sliding,
In the twisting weeds,
Pouncing, prancing,
Plotting privately
Murderous cat!

Heather Jardine (11)
St Mark's Primary School

THE RED-EYED CAT

The red-eyed cat crawls out at night
Trying to keep out of sight,
He pounces up and down with delight
Ready to scare the dog with a fright.

The red-eyed cat has teeth as sharp as nails,
Ready to scratch the cats' tails,
Of course the other cats think he's hell
And right they are about the red-eyed cat.

The red-eyed cat his tail so long
Whipping the other cats, singing a purring song,
The other cats bounce up and down
Screeching and screaming with a frown.

The red-eyed cat the frightener
The red-eyed cat a cat whipper
The red-eyed cat a teeth nasher
What sort of pet is that?

Jodie Cutler (11)
St Mark's Primary School

COLOUR POEM

A gem dancing in the bottom of a cave,
Some old broccoli mouldy with blue patches.
People from Ireland in shamrock green tops.
Instant grass sprouting out of the dark below.

Blood painfully moving onto the floor,
Lucozade the cold drink, seeping around the body,
Like a lava lamp blobbing around the glass rocket,
A silky moving jellyfish gliding in sunset seas.

Night with crystal stars in everlasting black-like sky,
As a shining pearl comes to a blank stop,
A fish diving deeper, deeper with every stroke.

Mist swirling and rising, like a rainy day,
With rain raining every second,
A new metal as strong as a cobweb swaying in the wind.

James Appleton (10)
St Mark's Primary School

BAINLY CAT

Bainly cat is always there in the silver moonlight
Waiting, waiting and then snuffling for a raging mouse fight.
Crescent eyes that watch like a targeted laser
And razor sharp claws beneath the prancing ginger legs.
Hot fiery fur burning,
And its sly tail whipping up the fog and dust.
Bainly cat bounces brilliantly across the bold black of the night.
In the lazy light of the day Bainly purrs in delight,
But as the dark of night falls Bainly's dappled skin burns bright
Until the morning light
When Bainly returns wearily to his warm cosy blanket.

Drew Duglan (10)
St Mark's Primary School

COLOURS

A volcano splatting, spitting out red hot boiling fireballs,
With bubbling lava running down the hard, black, holey, sizzling rocks.
Blood running red, squirming, squelching out of people's skin,
Slithering down arms and legs,
Pouring out like a red river flowing rapidly.
A tornado twisting, twirling all over the place,
Whipping, tearing, eating up everything in its path,
Moving from side to side like a ballerina.
Mars roaring red, swirling round and red with magnificent
                                              footprints all over it.
Twisting, twirling, bouncing up and down like a bouncing ball.

Trees swishing, swirling, swaying in the wind, in its own world
With its dark green leaves falling on the stony ground.
Seaweed swishing, swaying, swirling in the sea,
Bubbling, boiling, slithering in its way passing through
Smooth shells and hard stones, on the soft silky bed.
Frogs jumping, leaping happily into ponds,
Swimming swiftly through the water leaving ripples behind it,
Hiding in dark, creepy scary corners underneath rocks,
Like bats hanging in dark caves.
Snakes slithering, swiftly twisting, turning through the tall green
                                                pointy grass to camouflage it,
Scaly, silky, soft skin like human beings.

Dolphins swimming through the ocean sea passing through hard rocks,
Slimy seaweed and making funny and weird noises to other
                                                dolphins on its way,
Like whales communicating to each other.
A whale swimming.

Hannah Boughton (11)
St Mark's Primary School

The Lion's Tale

Maswoosh the lion was with might,
In the grass he's out of sight,
His tail it swipes the jungle ground,
Whilst hunting he never makes a sound.

Climbing trees and crouching low,
With stripes bright blazing, padding slow.
Purring mildly gently gasps,
Pounces with meat in his grasp.

His claws scratch the desert sands,
To forest creatures he's very grand!
He stands upon his rock and roars,
Above his head the eagle soars.

He prowls around his head held high,
His yellow eyes point to the sky.
His white teeth bared he strolls around,
His velvet paws upon the ground.

His whiskers wave in the air,
Those piercing eyes just look and glare,
His four paws pad till end of day,
When the sun is low and he's ate his prey.

He rests his shaggy mane and head,
Yawns, closes his eyes and goes to bed.

Emma Harrison (11)
St Mark's Primary School

The Lion

You never know when he'll lash out,
And you shouldn't hang about,
A furious killer and murderous too,
His eyes are the deepest colour blue.

By chance you might just slip away,
But watch, he'll follow all the way,
Do be scared and stay away,
That's the best idea I'd say.

But now will you ever know,
Not to scream and shout,
Just go!

Max Lovell (11)
St Mark's Primary School

My Cat

My cat is cute and playful
Friendly and cuddly too.
And he's always under the table,
But he doesn't go moo,
And the great thing is he plays peek-a-boo!

He's got sharp, raking claws,
On his big, fat, furry paws.
That's my cat, the one that dances to the song sung by The Corrs!

Kiran Patel (11)
St Mark's Primary School

COLOUR POEM

A dragon breathing fire, burning and melting the small tiny village.
Human blood dripping and spurting out of the cut arm.
Hot, flaming lava pouring and flowing out of the rocky volcano.
The planet Mars standing in the atmosphere like a snail moving as
                                        you don't notice every movement.
A jumping frog jumping from lily pad to lily pad.
An alien zapping humans as they pass in their shuttle.
Planet Venus swirling and twirling around to the Universe.
Green paint on a bedroom wall looked at with pride.
The sky shining as the light lights up the world.
A whale screaming his words to his fellow friends.
The ocean smashing and crashing against the hard rocky shore.
Planet Pluto freezing anything in its reach.
The sunset rising over the hilly hills.
The orange fruit sitting in a bowl waiting to be eaten.
Orange lilies blowing in the wind, pollinating each plant.
Orange cones on the road stopping each car driving into danger.

Oliver Hashtroudi (10)
St Mark's Primary School

PARENTS

Parents, what are they for?
They just sit around and look at the floor.
What goes on in their room?
Are they wizards with brooms?
I don't know, but I'd sure like to find out.

Parents, what are they for?
They just go around places breaking the law.
What do they buy with the money they make,
Or do they steal and take?
I don't know but I'd sure like to find out.

Parents, what are they for?
They just go out hunting for money and more.
What do they get up to when they're out on the town,
Or do they spend their money like drunken clowns?
I don't know but someday I will find out!

Danielle Lane (10)
St Mark's Primary School

GINGER

Ginger is a fluffy, friendly cat,
He has a miaow like a foghorn,
And eats just as noisily as a bird pecking away at birdseed.
Ginger is a funny, furry feline.
He can sit for hours watching us play, and never become bored!
What is he thinking?
He has a tear in his sensitive ear like a rip in my clothing,
And as I look into his sorrowful eyes - I feel sorry for him.
Where does he come from?
Quite often he has a fight on our territory
With the other cats in our area, and usually wins!
He lazes about in the gentle warmth of the sun
And rolls softly over onto his back, asking us to tickle his soft tummy.
As Ginger strolls along the garden patio like a newly-crowned king,
He looks like he has a bride's veil trailing behind him,
As leaves and twigs become caught in the curly hair at the
                                                    back of his legs.
His teeth are razor sharp, like giant stalactites hanging from a cave.
Ginger rubs his head against our legs as though he is telling
                        us 'Pet me' or 'I'm hungry.'
Ginger is cuddly, comforting and is a *purrfect* companion!

Brooke Zaidman (10)
St Mark's Primary School

COLOURS

Flutter, flutter butterfly,
As the rainbow shines so pink,
Ribbons blowing in the breeze,
As the mystery of the salty seas,
Brings the dragon up for air.

Evilness is a very strong colour,
Making blood flow like streams,
Hot flames, burning brighter,
Fear all around grows ever near.

Uncut grass, it blows in the wind,
Go is for the speedy and powerful cars to fly,
Fields are where the lovely little bunnies jump around,
Trees and meadows are part of what the colour is.

The sky is very rich and clear on a lovely sunny day,
A spaceship is sometimes this colour,
This is the food of some food colouring floating down in the jar.
I love this colour as it looks like the shimmering sea, guess the colour.

Kerry Short (10)
St Mark's Primary School

PICTURE

I close my door, I see . . .
A colourful procession marching through the crowded town,
Bands playing,
Dancers dancing.

I close my door, I see . . .
A UFO landing, its lights flashing, control board bleeping.
Aliens docking,
Lasers firing.

I close my door, I see . . .
Ghouls walking along a blood-stained corridor,
Ghosts spookily floating in and out of a wall,
A vampire biting someone painfully on the neck.

Thomas Bell (10)
St Mark's Primary School

MY CAT DODI

Chorus:
Cute and nice, furry and sweet,
My cat is the nicest you'll ever meet.

Big orange eyes, velvet paws,
He kills all those mice with those pointy claws,
Tickly whiskers, soft grey fur,
Listen very carefully you might hear him purr.

Chorus.

Creeping around the garden, stalking his prey,
Five mice, two frogs and a thrush a day,
He's not very patient, he always meows and meows,
And if he's really hungry, he'll show he wants it now.

Chorus.

If he's really happy, he'll rub against your feet,
And if you leave the sofa, he'll settle down in your seat.
But if he's really angry, you'd better stay away,
He can get quite vicious, you don't want to get in his way.

Chorus.

Kirsty Chant (11)
St Mark's Primary School

CAT, WALL, SUN

Cat.
Grey like cold smoke.
With his bright emerald eyes he sees a wall.
He pounces onto the wall and stretches.
His fur is just like a new soft carpet.

Wall.
His pigment blood red.
With yellow cement, like sand linking it all together.
Straight, smooth, sleek,
His outside is like the inside of a chestnut.

Sun.
Her body's gold like a coin,
Rolling out of a poor merchant's pocket,
Her mane like golden whips,
Cutting the Israelites' backs,
Big, beautiful, bright.

Melissa Lindsay (11)
St Mark's Primary School

DUDLEY THE RUNAWAY CAT

There was a cat called Dudley,
Who was fat and plump as a turkey.
He tried to run after the mice,
And thought this activity was quite nice,
And one day the mice ran away.

His mean eyes are like the moonlight,
Which sometimes gives you a fright,
His fur is as silver as the moon,
And his nose is as shiny and is the size of a spoon.

One day he tried to run away,
But his size got in the way,
He decided he was better off where he was,
Because there he would never last,
And would live to fight another day.

Marcus Whitmarsh (11)
St Mark's Primary School

THE TIGER

The tiger is a vicious predator
Sneaking around waiting to pounce on its prey,
Prey has been attacked
Eats it as quick as a vulture,
So other predators cannot eat his hard preparation catching it,
All that's left is the bones,
No meat is seen.

His orange stripes are like fire,
Beaming out brightly,
His black stripes are as black as the inside of a cave,
Standing out,
His eyes are as efficient as owls' eyes,
His jaws are a car jack,
Crushing everything.

He's a dangerous creature,
Ferocious, frightening, fast and fascinating.

So remember if you see the tiger lurking around . . .
Just run!

Jack Kane (10)
St Mark's Primary School

THE MIRROR

When I look into my mirror I see,
A shark swimming slyly trying to find its prey,
It suddenly smashes into some coral and
Catches sight of a fish for its lunch.

When I look into my mirror I see,
An Indian marching, singing and playing the drum,
Enjoying himself he realises lots of people are applauding him.

When I look into my mirror I see,
People dancing country and western style,
Going in and out with their partners,
Having a splendid time.

Leah Morgan (9)
St Mark's Primary School

THE SNOW LEOPARD

As the giant paw prints roam through the snows,
Five cuddly cubs stroll round her toes,
Her bushy white tail swishes in the breeze,
Like the wind blowing in the quivering trees,
Round and round she darts,
Like a thousand thumping hearts.
Her spotty white fur makes her look cuddly,
But really her cubs are even more snuggly,
They run round the crunchy ice,
Their little spots, like marks on a dice,
Their evil side is much more fierce,
Their huge teeth can easily pierce.
A big fluffy ear helps her to hear
And ensures she has nothing to fear.

Chloe Underwood (10)
St Mark's Primary School

THE LION

His raging mane swirling in the wind,
Like a whirlwind in an extreme storm,
His anger all wrapped up and tinned,
His fur as bright as a summer's morn.

His expression is timid and calm,
He has the world in his palm,
His hand is the wonder of this planet,
He came to this world and no one had to plan it.

The tempestuous grin on his face,
Makes you feel it's only you left in the human race,
He strolls round with not a care,
Whilst the wind blows his perfect, plush hair.

Where can I run?
Where can I hide?
I am still here four hours later, I ask
Where can I run?
And where can I hide?

Charlotte Muspratt (10)
St Mark's Primary School

MY FAVOURITE FEAST

For my fantastic feast I would have:
Super, sizzling Chinese chicken,
Served in a lake of sweet and sour sauce.
A colossal chocolate cake covered in cream,
Served on a crystal clear plate,
Big baked beans
Dished up on freshly baked toast.

Matthew Hall (10)
St Mark's Primary School

COLOURS

Blood dripped down the hungry, blood-thirsty hound's mouth,
While walking down the road leaving specks and drops of
                                                      blood behind.

The squeaming washing up liquid flowed down into the
                                      bubbling steaming water,
Leaving a slimy trail behind like a snail.

A puff of smoke filled the gloomy, smeary night sky,
A wizard appeared from nowhere.

The daffodils opened to see the day's sunlight.
And let out a gorgeous smell from their trumpets
As if a trumpet was playing.

Hannah Palmer (10)
St Mark's Primary School

MAGIC CUPBOARD

Inside my magic cupboard is a machine gun,
Blasting bullets rapidly like a rocket just about to take off.

Inside my magic cupboard is a sparkling, shining, turquoise waterfall,
Dropping over a hundred feet in the air.

Inside my magic cupboard is the Dead Sea
Crashing against the jagged rocks.

Inside my magic cupboard is a snake
Silently shivering through the long, pure, green grass.

Matthew Clark (9)
St Mark's Primary School

INSIDE MY MAGIC CUPBOARD

Inside my magic cupboard there's an Indian dancer,
Dancing outside the Taj Mahal in a silky dress.

Inside my magic cupboard there's a witch with a bubbling cauldron pot,
Putting strange creatures in one by one, waving her magic.

Inside my magic cupboard there's a lonely new forest foal,
Looking sad, weary and bewildered having just lost his mother.

Inside my magic cupboard there's a poor family
That's just won the lottery a week before Christmas, they're
                opening presents for the very first time.

Inside my magic cupboard there's a dolphin
Gliding through the blue barmy ocean with her newborn baby
                                close beside her.

Lauren Ostler (9)
St Mark's Primary School

MY FAVOURITE FANTASTIC FEAST

For my favourite, fantastic feast I would have:
A sizzling, frying, shining, glittering, bronze bowl
of small fish, to drool for.

For my favourite, fantastic feast I would have:
A silver dazzling plate with the most delicious, scrumptious
pepperoni pizza this world has ever seen!

For my favourite, fantastic feast I would have:
A mountain of chocolate ice cream as cold as the North Pole in a giant
golden gilded goblet.

Alex Barlow (9)
St Mark's Primary School

PICTURE

Glistening white snow,
Freezing cold on someone's toe.
Clouds drifting through the air
Lamp posts shining on the snow.

Evergreen trees,
Still have coats of leaves,
The sun shining on the snow,
Snow keeps falling at a flow.

Dogs bounding and jumping on grass,
The winter snow will soon pass,
Birds chirping in the winter cold,
Stop, stop I have been told.

The snow has now gone,
Oh no what have I done?
Let's go inside and have a cocoa
The snow is still freezing on my cold toe.

Eleanor King (10)
St Mark's Primary School

THROUGH MY MIND I SEE

Through my mind I see,
Waters flowing as blue as the sky,
Running blood just like a river,
Rocks that think like a brain.

Through my mind I see,
Help running past me,
Rocks hanging from the top,
People reminding me of the way.

Through my mind I see,
Wind blowing my hair,
Fine creatures tickling at my feet,
Blowing trumpets through my ears.

Through my mind I see,
Dancing in the disco,
Singing with my mind,
Hallelujahs round my mind.

Rebecca Airey (9)
St Mark's Primary School

COLOURS

Stars in the night sky,
Twinkling in someone's house,
Lava from a volcano spitting out
Like a snake spitting venom at you.

The sea twinkling in the night sky,
A bluebird singing a lullaby.
The sky at night.

Roses being given to you,
A sunset.
A person with a face all angry.

The sun at midday
Marigolds being given to you by someone special
The colour of a sports car racing.

Verity Younger (10)
St Mark's Primary School

WHEN I LOOKED IN THE WINDOW

I looked in the window and what I saw
Was spaceships fighting a galactic war.
Lasers flying everywhere,
Aliens not bothering to care.

I looked in the window and what I saw,
Was mermaids dancing on the ocean floor,
Sharks swimming swiftly after their prey,
The prey half dead, anyway.

I looked in the window and what I saw,
Was a volcanic eruption with lava beginning to pour,
All animals running for dear life,
Like a murderer running with his lethal knife.

I looked in the window and what I saw,
Was emerald countryside with flowers galore,
Butterflies, wasps and bumblebees,
Zoom around in the gentle breeze.

I looked in the window and what did I see?
Four beautiful paintings staring back at me!

Philip Watts (10)
St Mark's Primary School

I PEERED THROUGH THE MAGIC HEDGE

I peered through the magic hedge and I saw,
A garden as beautiful as the day,
A giant rose climbing and clambering its way up to the sun,
A tree swaying to and fro in the gentle breeze.

I peered through the magic hedge and I saw,
A great castle lake shimmering in the moonlight,
A mighty soldier riding off to war,
A princess with long golden hair locked up in an enchanted tower.

I peered through the magic hedge and I saw,
Mermaids and mermen having an enormous tea party in a coral house,
Otters playing hide-and-seek in the mass of seaweed,
Sharks' sharp teeth snapping at the air.

I peered through the magic hedge and I saw,
A ship sailing on the slashing sea,
Drunk seamen seeing sea monsters' shimmering, shiny scales.
Seals jumping off rocks into the midnight murky water.

Jemima Loveys (10)
St Mark's Primary School

AS I LOOKED THROUGH THE DOOR I SAW ...

As I looked through the door I saw,
A library full of people,
Towering with books,
Books wide and long, short and thin,
Stories and poems within.

As I looked through the door I saw,
A cheetah in the African plains, circling a herd,
Using its speed to catch its prey, and feasting on the kill.

As I looked through the door I saw,
A tornado thundering across the lawn,
Sweeping away everything in its path,
Forks of lightning and flashes of thunder,
A storm destroying all.

As I looked through the door I saw,
A shuttle in outer space,
Whizzing past the moon,
Glinting stars and wandering planets,
Giant, sweeping black holes.

Daniel McIllmurray (10)
St Mark's Primary School

OUT OF MY WINDOW

When I look out of my window I see:
Martians landing with lights surrounding their spaceship,
The spaceship is as red as fire,
Inside there are two green, ugly aliens from outer space.

When I look out of my window I see:
People swimming with dolphins,
The dolphins are blue and white,
And they swim along together perfectly.

When I look out of my window I see:
Stars floating in the midnight sky,
They are a rich yellow like a bag of gold,
They float like you are in space,
They twinkle beautifully.

When I look out of my window I see:
People dancing to the cancan,
They have their legs up really high,
They are as mad as a cat chasing a dog.

Lucy Lee (10)
St Mark's Primary School

CATS

Cats are sweet, cats are fun,
Cats are pleasant when they lay in the sun.

Cats are cute, cats are furry,
Cats are funny when they are really purrry.

Cats are lazy, cats are sleepy,
Cats are dozy and they are yawny.

Cats can catch things with ease,
Cats can withstand a breeze.

Cats can kill with an instant bite,
Cats stalk their prey mostly in the night.

Now the cats have been chased away,
By the evil dog wahey!

Stuart Lucas (11)
St Mark's Primary School

DETECTIVE

It was a dark night
As the shadow turned round the corner.
Round the dark gloomy corner in a beam of light.
A big beam of light,
A huge beam of light.

There was the detective,
The lonely detective.
He looked at the shadow,
The dark, ugly shadow
'I know what you did,
You did a terrible deed.
A horrible, spiteful deed,
And you know as well as I what it was.'
And with that the detective walked away.

Into the dark,
The dark,
The dark,
The dark.

Lauren Marsh (10)
St Mark's Primary School

IN MY EAR I HEAR

In my ear I hear dogs barking,
Their howling can be heard for miles,
Their paw steps shake the Earth,
They speak their own magical language.

In my ear I hear a lonely rat,
His feet are as wide as a ruler,
He has no friends to meet,
His teeth are as sharp as nails.

In my ear I hear a sad ghost,
Playing an abandoned piano,
Everyone is afraid of him,
But he is harmless to people.

In my ear I hear a scary bear,
His paws make giant ditches,
His roar scares people dead,
But he has tiny bears for friends.

Matthew Downton (10)
St Mark's Primary School

AS I PEERED THROUGH A CRACK I SAW

As I peered through a crack I saw,
Someone coming home over the hills,
On a weak horse but keeping a steady pace.
The golden rays of sunlight shining
And the shouts and screams from happy children.

As I peered through a crack I saw,
A big car chase right down the street,
Total mayhem as cars dashed to and fro,
Bang! Crash! Scrap metal everywhere.
Phew the thief's caught! Peace at last.

As I peered through a crack I saw,
The flowing waves and the silver moonlight,
Golden sand sparkling brightly,
Little sea creatures dancing in the water,
Shells with the sound of the sea,
Begging to be let out into the darkness.

Callum West (10)
St Mark's Primary School

IN MY MIND

In my mind I see,
Shadows creeping in the night,
Cellar stairs leading down,
A beastly horror film,
A dark wood in the middle of nowhere.

In my mind I see,
A Victorian picnic,
A child going on holiday,
A birthday with lots of presents,
Christmas Eve night.

In my mind I see,
An Indian festival,
Somebody playing bongo drums,
People in masks chanting,
An Indian chief starting a feast.

In my mind I see,
A violinist playing,
Beer being passed round,
People having a great time,
Cowboys line dancing.

Miles Chalkley (10)
St Mark's Primary School

PICTURES

I picked up a crayon and drew,
A knight in shining armour from the Round Table,
Rescuing a damsel in distress.

I picked up a crayon and drew,
A scaly dragon ransacking cities,
And setting houses alight.

I picked up a crayon and drew,
A foggy sea mist creeping ever higher,
And getting thicker every second.

I picked up a crayon and drew,
A rainforest buzzing with insects and animals,
With monkeys swinging through the trees.

Georgina Anderson (9)
St Mark's Primary School

MY FAVOURITE FEAST

In my golden, favourite, fantastic feast I would have:

Prawns swimming in enchanting chicken syrup,
Served in a baffling, boarded bowl.

A steaming marsh of magma pepperoni pizza,
Served in a sparkling silver gong.

Some deep fried barbecue ribs,
With a river of gravy on top.

A colossal ice cream,
Chocolate with peeled peanuts and chocolate chip dessert.
Served in a golden, gleaming goblet.

John William Cousin Arias (9)
St Mark's Primary School

THE DOOR

When I open my bright exciting door I see:
Men, black men riding upon greyish elephants,
Riding through the deep, dark jungle.

When I open my bright exciting door I see:
Aliens landing outside a girl's house
And opening the front door.

When I open my bright exciting door I see:
Talking fruit and vegetables dancing and twirling around
Around and around.

When I open my bright exciting door I see:
People of all ages partying in a wooden hut.

When I open my bright exciting door I see:
One very messy room.

Charlotte Cox (9)
St Mark's Primary School

WHY ARE OWLS KNOWN TO BE SO WISE?

Why are owls known to be so wise?
Why do wasps sting?
Why do bears have so much fur?
Why are some men called Sir?
Why can't animals speak?
Why is God so powerful?
Why is the sun so hot?
Why are fleas as small as dots?
Why do onions make us have tears?
Why are we here?

Georgia Vine (8)
St Martin's School

OFF TO SEA

People are saying goodbye to us,
Over the seas we go,
Everyone's saying goodbye to us,
As our ship prepares to go.

People are waving goodbye to us,
As we start to drift away,
Everyone's waving goodbye to us,
Wishing that we could stay.

People are crying and longing for us,
Hoping that we will survive,
Everyone's crying and longing for us,
Wondering if we're still alive.

People are shouting and cheering for us,
As the clock on the church strikes four,
Everyone's shouting and cheering for us,
As our ship approaches the shore.

Darcia George (10)
St Martin's School

THE WELL

Down, down, down I fell,
Into the water and into the well,
Splashed and showered with water I fell.
Where was I going? How could I tell?
Down, down and into the well.

'I'll take it, I'll take it' was all I could hear.
Who are they? I thought, shaking with fear.
I opened my eyes to take a little peer,
But what I could see was my worst fear,
For down beside me, two spirits appear.

Panting with fear, I finally awoke,
Was this real or was it a joke
Played by many cruel folk?
How would I ever know, if it was just a harmless joke?

Arvinder Athwal (10)
St Martin's School

MONTHS OF THE YEAR

January brings snow,
Which makes our hands glow.
February brings rain,
And that's a shame.
March brings sun,
Which is good for my mum.
April brings new life,
Time to marry my wife.
May brings Mary,
She is just like a fairy.
June brings good weather,
Then a bird grows a long feather.
July brings no school!
I'll swim in a relaxing pool.
August brings hot days,
I will go in the garden and gaze.
September brings falling leaves,
I won't fall and hurt my knees.
October brings scary things,
Like bats with huge wings.
November brings cold,
All over the world.
December brings Christ,
And the streams are all iced.

Kristina Guaggenti (8)
St Martin's School

CRAZY PLANE

My voyage is on a great old plane
A plane that's completely insane.
You'd have a great time I'm sure you would,
It was a crazy plane you wouldn't have understood.
So I'll tell you while I'm eatin' my pud.
A nasty man went on the plane,
A man cruel to poor and lame,
After he walked on the door slammed shut
And the plane went up, up, up!
The plane twisted and turned,
And as they went faster and faster
It was like butter being churned.
The crazy pilot had switched off automatic
And his curly hair was now static.
And when he had jumped off the plane
I can tell you one thing, he was not the same.
He jumped and skipped and hopped about
Like a fisherman who had caught the biggest trout
So after he had jumped off the plane
He was now good to poor and lame.

Alessandro Guaggenti (11)
St Martin's School

MY TOY SOLDIER

My toy soldier is under the bed,
He is next to my old ted.
He has a shiny gun,
That he holds across his tum.

He wears a suit,
But he is not that cute.
He has one leg with a boot on,
Some people say his name is Tom.

His brown, curly hair,
Is lovely and fair,
His eyes are so blue,
He looks straight at you.

My toy soldier is the best,
Better than the rest.
Sorry you are left under the bed,
Next to my old ted.

Gabriella Crouch (9)
St Martin's School

UNICORN

As I strolled through the snow-covered woods,
A strong gust of wind blew off my hood.
A rustling in the bushes made me feel rather scared,
So I went over to them to recover what was there.

As I pulled back the leaves,
Thinking of what it would be,
A pure white horse with crystal-like eyes,
Reared up its hooves in a fright of surprise.

As the winter sun glistened on its forehead,
I was surprised to see a horn instead.
A multi-coloured glittery horn,
It was to my surprise a unicorn!

This rare and beautiful animal,
I felt so lucky to see,
By tradition this fairy creature appears only to kings,
But here it was happening to me!

Jayde Morgan (11)
St Martin's School

SPACE

I jumped into a rocket,
And saw many electric sockets,
In front of me were dials and buttons,
I thought 'Oh no, I'd soon be mutton!'

A stew was not a pleasant thought,
It made my tummy go all taut,
It must be very stuffy and hot,
Stuck inside a cooking pot!

Swirling through space, intergalactic,
Just makes me feel, well asthmatic!
Claustrophobia, like sardines in a can,
Nearer the sun, but still no tan.

I want my bed; I want my teddy,
I want my water bottle ready.
Even Neil Armstrong having fun,
Was heard to yell, 'I want my mum!'

Leo Sharer (9)
St Martin's School

THE OLD MAN

I once saw an old man in the shops,
I suddenly saw him calling the cops,
I don't know why they came,
And the old man gave me the blame,
And all I wanted to do was go to the shops.

The next day I was walking to school,
And guess who I saw in the pool,
It was the old man,
He came over to me,
And blamed me for losing his key.

I ran back home,
And I knew where to go,
He followed me home,
And I picked up the phone,
And he was talking to my mum at home.

Ben Stanley-Clarke (11)
St Martin's School

THE CAT AND HIS PREY

The cat jumps over the fence
Creeping through the grass, his body tense,
Looking for a mouse with his intelligent eyes,
He snaps at all the flies
As he travels on his way.

At last he finds a mouse
And carries it into the house,
He gives it one more bite
You can barely stand the sight.

As he proudly plays with his prey,
His ears twitch
As he hears the light switch
Turn on
A human body appears.

He has no more time to play,
What will his master say?
No time to hide his precious gift
He must be swift
Or lose
His gift.

Sarah Shenton (9)
St Martin's School

MY FAMILY

My mum is sweet, my mum is kind,
Wherever I go she's never far behind.
When she is cross I cower away,
When she is happy we go out to play.

My mum plays tennis, she does very well,
She is very fit, she works with a lady called Mel.
My mum has friends, lots of them too,
She is so friendly, she will be friends with you!

My dad is great, my dad is fun,
He has two daughters and one son.
My dad is excellent at DIY,
And when he is fixing things, you never hear him sigh.

My dad is the manager of a hotel,
He looks after his wife and children as well.
My dad likes food, he likes chips the most,
But capping that all is cheese on toast.

My sister and brother are as good as gold,
They are seven and three birthdays old.
Georgia loves sweets, but they make her crazy,
Alexander's very lively, definitely not lazy.

My sister is blonde and very pretty,
The only thing she does not like our kitty.
My brother is fair and wide-eyed,
And absolutely loves bacon fried.

Now for me, the oldest child,
Sometimes I'm peaceful, sometimes I'm wild.
I'm ten years old and dark in colour,
And love very much my brother, sister, father and mother.

Sarah Moneypenny (10)
St Martin's School

THE MOUSE

There was a mouse
Who lived in a house,
Who lived under the floor.
The hole to his nest was just by the kitchen door.
Then the smell of cheese,
Drifted with ease,
To the hole where he sat by the door.
With a twitch of his nose,
He ceased his repose,
And he scampered across the floor.

He climbed up the table,
Which was not very stable,
And ran to the cheese on the plate,
The smell was so great
He thought he would faint,
As he nibbled away more and more.

He was full to the brim,
When the cat wandered in,
But as he was fat,
He could not run just like that,
So the cat nearly had a taste of him.
But to the cat's dismay,
He wriggled away,
And he made it back to tell the tale of his voyage.

Harri Lawrence (10)
St Martin's School

SCHOOL DAYS

I don't like Monday morning
It makes me feel so bad
People who keep yawning
Make me feel quite sad.

Tuesday is my worst day
Tests from Mr Tim
'Think, think, think!' I say
Then I forget to give my homework in.

Hooray, hooray, it's Wednesday today
Halfway to the weekend
Computer all morning, it's time to play
And I can sit with my best friend.

Thursday we wear tracksuits
And walk down to the pool
Alexander forgot his swimsuit
In his pants, he'll look a fool.

Friday morning, nearly there
I'll make it through the week
'Only two days off, it's just not fair!'
The whole class began to shriek.

Alice Carden (9)
St Martin's School

PETS

Small pets, large pets, big or small,
Fluffy ones, hairy ones, or even ones that crawl!
Pets that climb, pets that hide or pets that talk,
Pets that dance, pets that sing or ones that walk!
Dogs that bark or cats that purr,
Or pets that are friends and like to dance,
And like to do a show!

Funny dogs, naughty cats and cheeky rabbits,
The ones that are the best and have a few habits!
Silly ones, or naughty ones or ones that like to have fun,
Or even heavy ones that weigh nearly a ton!
Cute ones, or cuddly ones, but I like them all!
But my favourite ones are cute and very, very small.

Emily Wilson (8)
St Martin's School

POETIC VOYAGES

Today Sam hopped on a ship.
He was off on a very long trip.
The ship left the bay
Without a delay,
And the passengers all said 'Hooray!'

He ran on top of the deck,
There was a sharp pain in his neck,
He collapsed on the floor,
Just next to a door,
And suddenly felt nothing more.

When he woke up,
He was sick in a cup,
Then went off to bed,
With a bump on his head,
And said 'Why am I not home instead?'

At last they reached the dock.
Sam turned and looked at his clock.
It said half-past three,
He fell on his knees,
Then hurried off home with glee.

Luke Naveira (10)
St Martin's School

MY WEEK

Hip, hip, hooray! It's Saturday today,
I get to play for all of the day.

Gymnastics on Sunday,
It's really my fun day.

Monday we have a test,
Which isn't the best.

Tuesday brings joy,
Because we draw a toy.

On Wednesday a story we write,
About flying my kite.

Thursday to the pool we walk
And to our friends we talk.

Friday I have singing,
I can hear the bells ringing
For tomorrow is the weekend!

Hannah Whiteside (8)
St Martin's School

WHY ARE WE HERE?

Why do people come and go?
Why does our hair grow?
Why do we need to eat?
Why do we write and read?
Why can't animals speak?
What were we made from?
Why are we here?

Leyla MacDonald (9)
St Martin's School

POETIC VOYAGES

P eople watch and wave goodbye.
O nly mothers are filled with dread.
E ndless sea beneath endless sky,
T hat is what lies ahead.
I mages of loved ones will never die.
C omforting memories stop tears being shed.

V enturing far, slowly we roam.
O ver the seas, there is no one there.
Y et we know we are not alone.
A nd every one of us share
G reat dreams of our real home
E very one of us knows
S oon we'll be back, soon we'll be home.

Lauren Harvey (11)
St Martin's School

OH WHY?

Why are the seas so blue?
And why do we get the flu?
How long will Earth stay in space?
And will anything ever take its place?
Why do we have colours like pink, blue and red?
And why, oh why do we have to go to bed?
Why is the world round? I don't see why
And why can't we rise up and fly?
Why do leaves turn brown and fall?
I do not know the answers at all.

Blue Müller (8)
St Martin's School

OUR WORLD

How does our hair grow?
How do balloons float with air?
How do cheetahs run with skinny legs?
Where is paper sold from?
How do trees grow so big?
How long will the sun stay in space?
How do birds fly so high?
Why do tornadoes damage towns?
Why do we go to school?
How do oranges get their juice?

Alex Harvey (8)
St Martin's School

CITY'S QUESTIONS

How does rubbish get recycled?
How do birds fly in the sky?
How do fish eat under water?
Why would a crab pinch you hard?
Why don't we speak every language?
How is bread made into a sandwich?
Why call corridors sometimes halls?
How does ivy grow up walls?

Lauren Harley (9)
St Martin's School

The Jungle

There was an old monkey who sat in his chair,
And wondered about his life in the jungle,
He picked up his pipe and blew with his might
And then came a small little bubble.
Pop, went the bubble and then he heard a knock.
But when the monkey opened the door,
Who did he see but his friend Al Gore.
'5, 4, 3, 2, 1,' he said,
Sorry I'm going back to bed.

Christopher Parsons (8)
St Martin's School

Why?

Why are lemons so sour?
Why are apples so crunchy?
Why do we write with a pencil and pen?
Why do we live in a house?
Why do we save up money in the bank?
Why do our teeth fall out?
Why do salmon jump out of the water?
Why isn't there a pot of gold at the end of a rainbow?

James Frearson (8)
St Martin's School

TRAVELLING

A car journey, so long and boring I feel like my brain is sawing.
I wish I could fly on a magic horse,
And travel all over the world.
I also wish car journeys weren't so uninteresting!
And why do we have to go by car?
Why can't we ride on an aeroplane instead?
And visit Africa, China, America, Australia, Malta, Japan.
And maybe Heaven!
We might even get stranded and end up in a tropical paradise,
Surrounded by a clear blue sea and sandy beaches with palm trees!
And we could live there for all eternity.
Travelling is so much fun,
If you don't have to go in a car that is!

Laura Begeman (8)
St Thomas Garnet's School

ME AND MY ADVENTURE

When I was at the end of the rainbow
There was no pot of gold
I asked the shopkeeper at the end of it
And he said it had all been sold.

And in my plane I thought I would go to St Ives
And guess what I saw, a man with seven wives.

And on my rollerblades over the ramps
In the end I just got too much cramp
And me in bed with my big bright lamp.

And me on my surfboard
And my dad in his Porsche!

Samuel Plank (8)
St Thomas Garnet's School

The School Trip

We are on the school trip
And I am sitting in the ship,
Which isn't much fun,
I nibble at my bun.
My mum tells me to share my sweets,
I go and sit on a rock and watch a fleet of ships go by.
Then the teacher calls me and I get pulled by the tie.
We are given a quiz to do,
Then I see a whale go by and she warns me
I will fail if I don't work at it.
When the quiz is over I lurk about in the trees,
The sun hurts my eyes.
And the flies aren't much help, they are worse.
Only another hour till we go home and I can forget today happened
And just relax and drift off to bed.

Theresa Gillings (10)
St Thomas Garnet's School

A Voyage To The Moon

Climbing in a rocket, saying goodbye to Earth.
Then comes the countdown, 3, 2, 1, zoom!
Flying through a starry sky,
Through the night we carry on the flight.
As fast as a motorbike,
As powerful as a volcano,
Then we land on the moon.
A rocky ball as thick as a brick
But after that I felt sick.

Tom Weston (8)
St Thomas Garnet's School

SMUGGLING

We're going on a voyage
We don't know what to see or do
Will it be aboard a pirate ship
Or whizzing round space in a flying saucer?

We began aboard the pirate ship
Smuggling lions back to Kitty Island
We swapped the coins to save the golden parrot
The pirates realised that they were chocolate coins
And we made a lucky escape in the flying saucer.

In the flying saucer
We crossed the Dead Sea
Whizzing round the world to return
Just in time for tea.

Brookeleah Gossling (9)
St Thomas Garnet's School

OUR YACHT THE GREY MOUSE

As we sail from Poole Quay,
There are so many islands and of course salt sea!
The rudder swings, the sails swirl,
And look the spinnaker is being unfurled.
I love being on The Mouse . . .
A storm? Oh no this cannot be!
Not now in the middle of the sea.
Look at the waves caused by the wind,
Now the sails will have to be trimmed!
It's a pity that we have to moor,
Goodbye Mouse . . . but just for now,
As my family's spirit you shall always allow.

Bethany Wildeman (10)
St Thomas Garnet's School

THE JOURNEY TO SEASHELL ISLAND

I was sailing on a rocky ship
With my blood-thirsty crew.
I shouted 'Pull up the anchor
And out up the sails!'
We were going to Seashell Island.
It was a long voyage to the island
We went through storms and half of my crew died.
We got attacked by a pirate ship,
And then a deadly storm came.
Our sail toppled over on fire
The ship sunk, deck first,
And I sunk to the bottom of the ocean.
Then a red cloud covered the ocean
And sucked me in,
And I landed on Seashell Island
And my crew drowned.

Harry Brown (8)
St Thomas Garnet's School

GOING ON HOLIDAY

I was on a plane
And got a bad pain
I was walking up the aisles
And heard somebody say we have been there miles
I saw a girl be sick
And heard a clock go tick
When we were there we got in a car
And went past a bar
I heard the rustling leaves
I heard my mum's rattling keys.

Rachel Gillings (8)
St Thomas Garnet's School

IT'S SO UNFAIR

It's so unfair, if you're a child,
Grown-ups saying:
'You can't do this,'
'You can't do that.'
It's so unfair, if you're a child.

If it's raining outside,
I want to be out there,
But there's the grown-ups saying:
'You aren't allowed out
And that's final!'

If you want to watch TV
There's always a grown-up saying:
'What about tidying your room?'
It's so unfair, if you're a child.

When I'm grown-up
I'm going to be kind
I'm going to let my children do what they want,
But right now I'll have to put up with it,
Oh no! Mum's found out; work time because she's cross.
It's so unfair, if you're a child.

Help! She's found me!

Rachel Dingley (10)
St Thomas Garnet's School

JOURNEY TO THE MOON

We're on a journey to the moon,
Let's not waste any time and be off soon.
Make it snappy, let's go quick,
Before our parents have a fit.

Our rocket is ready to launch in the sky,
Our seatbelts are fastened, we are ready to fly.
I'm feeling very nervous at what we might find,
Up and away in the darkest of night.

Sam Ring (9)
St Thomas Garnet's School

MY NEW ROOM

The moment had come,
Oh what fun!
My room was to be decorated,
By my mum.
Now you must understand,
She's not that dab hand,
I wanted it to be bright,
But didn't want to give everyone a fright!
I chose the colour mango,
So that my friends and I could tango!
I said I'd help her,
And at first she was pleased,
But I soon discovered,
There was more to this than ease.
The sun, the moon and the stars,
Shone on the wall,
These were definitely not going to fall.
I was covered from head to toe,
I stood at the door saying
'Friend or foe!'
What a great day,
What a great mum,
A job, you will agree,
Very well done!

Olivia Johnson (7)
St Thomas Garnet's School

DREAMING

I would love to wake up in the morning
And see everything all white
Because that's what I dream of
Every single night.

I would love to catch the snowflakes
Falling from the sky
And build a great big snowman
Ten feet high.

I would love to have a snow fight
With my cousin Jill
And go and get my sledge
And race it down the hill.

I suppose I'll have to wait
Until next year
And keep on having dreams
Until the snow appears.

Toby Khalife (9)
St Thomas Garnet's School

BOATS

Going on a boat to France,
I'm so happy I would like to dance!
I can't wait to get there,
Because my mum told me we could go to a fair.
I would love to drive the boat, it would be so fun,
When we get there, out comes the sun.

    Now we have arrived,
    We can have a great time!

Amy Coppini (9)
St Thomas Garnet's School

THE SHIP

The ship sailed across the sea,
Crashing and smashing on the waves so high,
That nearly touched the sky.

The ship sailed across the sea,
While the rain pelted down across the decks,
The sea was rough but not tough enough.

The ship sailed across the sea,
The wind was strong, as strong as could be,
The wind blew very, very strong and pushed the ship along.

The ship sailed across the sea,
The waves smashed the ship into the rocks 'Crash!'
It was a horrendous sound as the ship sank.

Liam Cosgrove (11)
St Thomas Garnet's School

SAILING

Sailing across the bay,
On a bright summer's morning,
Looking at the view,
It never gets boring.
Swishing about in my little boat,
I never sink,
I stay afloat.
The nice big splashy water,
Splashing over my rear quarter.
The wind blows my jib,
The name of my boat is Spare Rib.

Philippa King (7)
St Thomas Garnet's School

DESERT ISLAND

Going over waves like a roller coaster ride,
Splashing, crashing, dashing,
Going really fast with a big motor jet,
Splashing, crashing, dashing.

Spot land in the distance,
Going full speed,
Get onto the desert island,
Brumming, bashing, bumping.

Find a site to eat some food,
Make a house of wood,
Get into the boat, drive back home,
Splashing, crashing, dashing.

Oliver Porter (9)
St Thomas Garnet's School

JAPAN

When I want to go somewhere,
I close my eyes and think,
I want to go to Japan,
Very, very quick.

I see ladies in kimonos,
And sandals on their feet,
In their hair they wear flowers,
And they look very sweet.

When it's time for supper,
I close my eyes and think,
I want to go to Pizza Express,
Very, very quick.

Isabella Clark (9)
St Thomas Garnet's School

IN THE JUNGLE

Trekking through the jungle,
What did I see?
A big hairy monkey staring at me.

Walking through the jungle,
What did I hear?
The roar of a lion, sounded very near.

Creeping through the jungle,
What did I touch?
A scaly snake, didn't like it very much.

Jogging through the jungle,
What did I smell?
Don't know what it was but I ran like hell!

Rose Weston (11)
St Thomas Garnet's School

CREATURES

Creatures of the world I see,
Come, come, come to me.

Birds, bees, foxes and fleas,
Fishes and dolphins and things in the seas.

I love little creatures,
With sweet little features.

Creatures, creatures everywhere,
I give them all the love and care.

Creatures of the world I see,
Come, come, come to me.

Grace Garrett-Sadler (11)
St Thomas Garnet's School

SPRING

My favourite season is spring,
Because of plants and things.
I like the daffodil most,
And the bluebells by the coast.
I just love spring,
Because of plants and things.

Colours of spring are so great,
You must enjoy it at this rate.
I love spring
Because of plants and things.

I normally take a bicycle ride,
To get some fresh air outside.
Oh! I love spring,
Because of plants and things.

I love it when the sun goes down,
There's a good view in town.
I just adore spring,
Because of plants and things.

Maeve Dunne (8)
St Thomas Garnet's School

MY CAT SNOWY

I have a cat called Snowy
Her colours are grey and white,
Her eyes are a beautiful yellow
And we love her with all our might.

She's sometimes very naughty
When she catches a bird or two
But eventually we forgive her
Because that's what all cats do.

She scratches on the furniture
And we all get very cross
But when we try to stop her
She wants to be the boss.

We wouldn't be without her
Because she's really very sweet
But we all agree on one thing
She's the best cat in the street.

Jana Browne (8)
St Thomas Garnet's School

HOLIDAYS

Yippee, I'm going on holiday!
Where should I go?
To a theme park with lots of roller coasters?
Or a hiking holiday and get my boots muddy?

Perhaps I'll go skiing in Austria,
Or just relax on a beach in Spain!
Swim with dolphins,
Or just go to Rome and see the history.

I could go to Switzerland
And taste their chocolate,
Or go on a cruise and enjoy the luxury!
Maybe I'll visit New York and
Shop, shop, shop.
I can't decide.
Maybe I'll just stay at home!

Laura Johnson (10)
St Thomas Garnet's School

ALIENS

Aliens, aliens are they true?
What colour are they,
Green or blue?
Are they up there
In the sky,
Waiting for me to die?
Do they have eyes like
Snakes or cats?
Or is it a lie, how about that?
Are they skinny, big or fat?
Or do they have a pet that looks like a bat?
What powers do they have?
Do they travel in spaceships and
Will they ever come to Earth?
Do they go to work or just float around?
And do they have brothers and sisters too?
Aliens, aliens up there or not?

Kapil Chauhan (7)
St Thomas Garnet's School

KALE

There was a young postman from Frail
Whose unfortunate name was Kale
He got teased day and night
For his name wasn't right
That poor young postman named Kale.

In order to deliver the mail
He would board a boat and sail,
So despite his name
He received lots of fame
Until he went down in a gale.

From the surface to the bottom floated Kale
Who was spied by a large hungry whale
So into the sea, he became the whale's tea
And no one received any mail!

Emily King (9)
St Thomas Garnet's School

MY AUNTIE PAT

Shh! Don't tell anyone,
But my aunt's an alien.
I first noticed last week,
She came round ours,

When everyone wasn't looking
She took all the food off the table
And, oh well, this bit's too horrible.
OK, well she ate it all in one minute,
Everyone blamed it on me.

Then the thing bled from
All different places,
I said it was the rabbit.

Well next time she came round,
I told her what I had seen.
Then the thing said,
'Oh didn't you know you're one too?'
So now we're all
Aliens.

Catherine Hixson (9)
St Thomas Garnet's School

SUSIE

Susie is the name of my cat
She likes to sit on the doormat
She is black and quite tiny
Her eyes are always shiny.
When we get home late
She runs indoors and looks for her food
And when she sees none,
She gets in a mood.
After she's eaten she washes her fur
Then jumps on my lap and begins to purr.
Sometimes she's lively and plays with her toys
She's always liked girls but is not keen on boys.
I love my cat, she's special to me,
That's why I tickle her when she's on my knee.

Kristy O'Donnell (8)
St Thomas Garnet's School

DREAMS

Sometimes when I go to bed and try to sleep,
I wake up in the night with a nasty fright.
I dream of funny faces all around me,
I put my head under the cover and wish they would go away.
But the shadows dance in front of me.
I call out for Mummy who comes rushing up,
She says 'Don't be silly, it's only a dream, go back to sleep.'
No more nasty dreams I hope.

Kamilah Hassan (8)
St Thomas Garnet's School

Rocky

His eyes are as dark as a winter's night
His shell a home from any fright
He lives his life with lazy days
And cares for nothing except his own ways.

We may think he's slow and old
But really he is brilliant and bold
Gently basking in the glow of his heat
Asking nothing, but simply to eat.

I know he can hear me when I whisper his name
His head bobbing gently, not knowing his fame
He's clever and majestic, but never cocky
He's my special friend, my tortoise Rocky.

Tom Flynn (9)
St Thomas Garnet's School

Colour Poem – Yellow

The yellow sun shining on the yellow daffodils as they blow
                                                                      in the breeze,
And the yellow light shining in the houses as night falls.

The yellow sunflowers in the garden, smiling and nodding their heads,
The buttercups in the field twinkling, reflecting the sun's rays.

The yellow fluffy chicks like tiny flecks of gold running to and fro,
The farmer with his tractor driving through the sea of
                                                    rustling yellow corn.

Connor Rockey (8)
St Thomas Garnet's School

In The Jungle

I walked through the jungle; when I saw a big bear,
I ran for my life, whilst gripping my hair.
I could hear my heart thumping,
My throat had gone dry,
But I did not dare to sit down and cry.

Oh no, there's a snake slithering along,
It mustn't see me before I am gone.
My hands were now shaking,
My legs had gone numb
What other frights were next to come?

I now see a lion heading my way,
Big, fat and fearsome, and I am his prey.
My hair is on end,
My teeth are clenched tight,
Thank heavens I've been dreaming during the night.

Natalie Rondeau (9)
St Thomas Garnet's School

My Eccentric Grandpa

One day I saw my grandpa looking in our shed,
I asked him what he was doing and this is what he said:
'I'm making a new invention that will finally rule the world.
So never fear my dear, it's like all the others,
So go inside and quickly tell your mother
That it's not a flowery vase (or something that costs as much)
It's not a dictionary or a candle holder, as such,
In fact it's a . . .
Fly swatter!'

Francesca Welsh (10)
St Thomas Garnet's School

WHY?

Why oh why does my mummy always say 'Brush your hair'?
Because I do not think it's fair.

Why, oh why does my daddy say 'Put your clothes away'?
I want to watch TV and play.

Why, oh why does my nanny say 'You must eat your greens'?
Can't I do my Britney routines?

Why, oh why does Grampy say 'It's time to go to bed'?
I'd rather read a book instead.

To be ordered around, is this my fate?
Or perhaps it's because I'm only eight!

India Hall (8)
St Thomas Garnet's School

HOLE IN ONE!

It is Saturday morning, hip, hip, hooray!
Do I go to school? No way!
I'm out on the golf course today.

Helping my dad load my bag in the car,
Luckily my golf club is not too far.

Driving through the park, it's a beautiful sunny day,
I'm soon on the golf course, hip, hip, hooray!

I hit my first ball, what a great shot,
Will it land on the green? Maybe not.

Just a minute everyone is looking my way,
Shouting 'It's a hole in one!' Hip, hip, hooray.

George Soan (9)
St Thomas Garnet's School

TRAVEL

Should I travel by plane?
Should I travel by train?
Should I travel like a witch
On a flying broomstick?
Should I travel by car?
But not too far.
Should I travel by bike?
Or should I do a hike?
Should I travel by foot,
Or just stay put?
Should I travel by horse,
Along a golf course?
Should I travel by scooter
With a big hooter?
Should I travel by skates
With all my mates?
Should I travel . . .

Jamie Rickard (10)
St Thomas Garnet's School

IF I HAD A DOG

If I had a dog,
It would be lots of fun,
I would take him to the park,
And he would run, run, run.

If I had a dog,
He'dg331
 have a black, wet nose
Soft golden fur
And eyes that glow.

If I had a dog
I'd play with him every day
I would teach him to fetch a ball
And tell him to stay.

If I had a dog
I'd walk him in any weather
Sun, rain, wind or snow
He would be my friend for ever.

Amy Spencer (7)
St Thomas Garnet's School

NIGHT FRIGHT

In the night the moon is bright,
I saw a star and it was alight.

I turned round and saw a fox,
It frightened me right out of my socks

I ran and ran into the night
I saw an owl just out of sight.

I watched it swoop down to the ground
To see it grab what it had found.

I didn't like the sight I saw
So I ran and ran back to my door.

I opened up and went inside
And there I promised not to go outside.

Sophie Skinner (7)
St Thomas Garnet's School

OH BROTHER!

My brother is really a pain!
Often you'd think he was insane.
He starts acting stupid, you'd think he had no brain.
He starts running down the lane,
Instead of playing with our Great Dane.

He messes about with a wail and a shout.
Mum gets so cross
She gives him a clout.

Though, when I stop and think
I should be fair
I tease him too,
And drive him to despair.

When all is said and done
He is my best friend,
And my number one.

Liam O'Leary (8)
St Thomas Garnet's School

SKIING

Down the slopes
I go on my skis,
And just to go faster, I bend my knees.
I hit a bump
I fly in the air,
I land with a wobble,
A shake and no cares,
I pick myself up and away I go,
I'm off to the chairlift for another go!

Todd Lewis (9)
St Thomas Garnet's School

A WET, WET DAY

Splish-splash, splish-splash,
That's how the rain goes.
Splish-splash, splish-splash,
And drops off the end of my nose.

Pitter-patter, pitter-patter,
On my daddy's head.
Pitter-patter, pitter-patter,
'I'm getting wet,' he said.

Drip-drop, drip-drop,
From the sky all misty and grey.
Drip-drop, drip-drop,
At last I can go out to play.

Joshua Harris (7)
St Thomas Garnet's School

MY IMAGINATION

It was a wonderful day
A girl played in the hay
I say
It looks like Kay.

In May
I made clay
I went on a sleigh
And found out I was in a play.

I heard a neigh
Move out of my way
But it just lay
In display.

Ross Browne (9)
St Thomas Garnet's School

TRAVELLING

Uncle Pete is taking his family for a treat.
Connie and Bonnie,
But what about Ronnie?

Gill and Lil,
But what about Dill?

Their adventure begins on a bike,
That they really like.
It's pink and blue and green too.

They travel to . . .

Africa to South Africa,
North Africa, West Africa.

That's where it ends,
They're still travelling today.
They're in books such as ours!

Disa Daly (9) & Chloe Seaward (10)
Stourfield Junior School

THE TRAIN VOYAGE

Faster and faster the train whistles by
As the smoke flies up in the sky.
The fields are vast.
With the moles digging holes in the grass.
I hear the raindrops fall.
Then I hear a weird call
It was the train driver saying 'Cor'.
It was amazing what we saw.

Bethany Hawker (10) & Georgia McKinney (9)
Stourfield Junior School

THE LIT UP NIGHT

Sailing through the lit up night,
I saw a stunning sight,
As I went closer the birds began to sing,
They sang 'Save, save our king.'

I shouted 'Alright, I'll bring back your king,'
I jumped on the bird's wing
And realised that was the wonderful sight,
I knew I was doing everything right.

As I flew over the sea,
We stopped on a tiny tree.
After that I found myself back on the boat,
Luckily I stayed afloat.
Just me on my own,
Me all alone.

Yasmin Philpott (9)
Stourfield Junior School

MY OLD GRANDPA

My old Grandpa travelled far,
In his Californian car.
It was fast but also vast.
My old grandpa could hardly drive,
So he crashed into a beehive.
The bees got mad and tried to stab.
Grandpa got stung pretty bad.

My old grandpa travelled far,
In his multi-coloured car.
It was cool but not that small.
Everyone loves the brand new car.

Nick Sumbler & Sam Excell (9)
Stourfield Junior School

THE SHOPPING SPREE

An egg box in Tesco the mouse lived in,
When the mouse, she heard a terrible din,
'These free-range eggs look really great,
They're very small and light-weight.'

'Ekk!' screamed the woman as she opened the box,
'Help!' squeaked the mouse 'It's an ugly fox!'
Before the mouse could grab her dolly,
She fell into a shopping trolley.

The shopping trolley with the squeaky wheels,
Was heading for the checkout tills,
Then, as quick as a gunshot,
Mousey dived into a yoghurt pot.

The yoghurt pot rolled off the counter,
The checkout lady said 'Sir, have a free voucher.'
Suddenly the pot sped through the air,
Kicked by a banker with bright red hair.

The banker was drinking a bottle of gin,
While Mousey landed in a baked bean tin,
The baked bean tin was labelled 'lunch',
Mouse cried, 'Help! I'm for the crunch.'

But Mouse came out the tin alive,
By distracting the cleaner doing a jive,
The cleaner put Mousey back in her box,
Far, far away from the ugly fox.

Rebekah Oliver (10)
Stourfield Junior School

DREAMY VOYAGE

It started when I bumped my head,
So my mum told me to go to bed,
I fell asleep within a tick,
And found myself upon a brick.
I jumped right off and ran a mile,
And found myself in the river Nile.
I saw a boat,
Which was afloat,
There was a pharaoh,
Who was eating an Aero.

I asked him for a tiny bit,
He said 'No', but gave me a lick.
I carried on floating in the sky,
Saw Cleopatra and said 'Hi'.
Then I saw land,
That was drenched in sand.
As I got closer
I saw a mini toaster,
Which was next to a mini man,
Who was in a rock band.

He was very glad,
To be rescued from the bad,
So he rose up in a tiny bubble,
And said his name was Mr Trouble.
I asked him why,
He said 'I kill flies'.
I replied 'That's good'
And that he should.
This is where my voyage ends,
Because now I've found my special friend.

Charlotte Ponton & Rudi Barwis (9)
Stourfield Junior School

MY TRIP AROUND THE WORLD

At last the day came
I was so excited as I boarded the plane.
We took off with great speed
And climbed to the clouds.
The engines roared and became very loud.
It won't be long now till we arrive in Rome.
I'm glad I'm with my friends,
At least I won't be alone.

So much to see, so much to do.
I will throw my three coins into the fountain,
And make a wish or two.

Then we're off to Paris,
A city of dreams,
Where the air is so fresh and the streets are so clean.

We all climb the Eiffel Tower,
And look out at the gardens with all their wonderful flowers.

Then as we flew over the white cliffs of Dover,
I knew my holiday was finally over!

Scott Nicol & Adam Salih (10)
Stourfield Junior School

BACK TO THE FUTURE

Riding through time, back to the past
I wonder how long my voyage will last
All I can see are flashes and stars
I can also see some other time cars.

I'm back in the past, what can I see?
Look there it's me as a baby
I have to carry on, this journey's such fun
And soon my travelling will be done.

Back to the time of the wild, wild west
I think this stop will be the best!
It's getting late, I must go home
I don't like it all alone.

Back at home, Mum asks me where I'd been
So I told her all the things I had seen
I really liked the cowboy men
I wish I could go back again!

Amanda Shonfeld (10)
Stourfield Junior School

JUNGLE

When I go through the jungle, in the meadow green grass
I don't know what will come, I don't know what will pass!
Tigers ready to pounce on me.
The crow looks at my shiny key.
Koala bears live in trees
They strike at the helpless bees
There's a little pond, crystal clear,
There's piranha fish, that's what I fear.
The crocodile is letting his eyes go astray
Beware! Beware! Just keep away.
I look around,
I hear lots of sound
I hear the hissing of the snakes
My arms are slightly beginning to ache.
I'm trembling in my bones
I really feel like ice cream cones
I'm out of this jungle place
Thank goodness I don't have to see
That tiger's face!

Hannah Witcombe (9)
Stourfield Junior School

TRAVEL

Modern travel is a funny thing.
You really don't know where to begin.
For example the electric train.
It really is such a pain!
Their schedules are hardly ever on time,
The managers couldn't give a dime.
Jet planes are not so roomy.
So everyone feels very gloomy.
Why should people go first class?
After all they're one of us.
Another thing the cars are so bumpy
And that makes people very grumpy.
That is all of my horrid groans,
And quite a lot of my moans.

Matthew Sloane (9)
Stourfield Junior School

THE JOURNEY

I went on a journey
Far, far away,
Right next to the soft, smooth bay.
Every morning when I woke up,
I would take a shiny, clean cup,
I poured myself a cup of tea,
And looked out of the window at the sea.

The sea was like snowflakes falling from the sky,
I just don't want to say goodbye.
The leaves shuffled in the breeze,
Underneath the tall, dark trees.

Rebecca Sheppard (10)
Stourfield Junior School

IN THE ROCKET

10 - I climb into my enormous white spacesuit.
9 - I place my plastic fish bowl like helmet on my head.
8 - We enter the lift and rise up to the cabin.
7 - I feel my hands shaking from nerves.
6 - Switch on the computer, green and red lights shine out.
5 - My heart is pounding like I am in a boxing match.
4 - I check the supplies for the long journey ahead.
3 - I climb into the seat.
2 - I strap myself in tightly.
1 - Frozen with fear, I hold on tight.

Blast Off!

Katie Guy (10)
Stourfield Junior School

THROUGH THE SANDY DESERT

Through the sandy desert I hear nothing.
All I can hear is the sliding of sand snakes,
And the whistling of the wind.
There is no sight of a drop of water,
Still no signs of another man,
My feet are getting very tired,
And I need my sleep.
Suddenly I hear a noise,
But it is a beetle at my feet.
I have nothing to worry about,
So I go back to sleep.
When I go back to sleep,
My heart is pounding like thunder,
When I wake up, still no man in sight.

Francesca Affleck (9)
Stourfield Junior School

COMPUTER COURSE

There once was a boy trapped in a PC,
In there with his mum and his family,
It was not very nice, it was stuffy and hot,
He kept getting viruses and felt ill a lot.
He soon decided to go on a quest,
To find a way out, to try his best.
He set off to find the witch called Ursula Urse,
Who put on them this horrible curse.
He declared he would follow the yellow wire cable,
To get seen on the screen if he was able.
But first they would have to play a clever, sly trick,
If they wanted to succeed they would have to be quick.
A message on screen would have to appear,
It would have to be bold and very clear.
The plan was that the witch would see,
And follow the instructions so they could flee.
The witch would have to put in a disk,
If she didn't it would be a terrible risk.
They'd make their way to the hard disk drive,
And have to be quick to stay alive.
They all jumped down when the draw flew out,
The witch gave out a frightened shout,
It was so exciting that with the opening of a drawer,
They found themselves back on their living room floor.
The witch disappeared for evermore,
Although you never can be sure.

Jessica Brankin (9)
Stourfield Junior School

TITANIC

As I gazed over the crystal, glistening sea,
I felt a deep, cool breeze inside me.
There stood the girl that set fire to my heart,
She was a huge flame, a great piece of art!
Then she shimmied to the edge,
And she stepped onto the wooden ledge,
She then stepped over the metal rail,
Her beauty had made me trail.
Then I combed my fingers through her hair
She then shook her head in despair.
She let one hand off the rail.
I then said 'You're not for sale,'
I pulled her back and lifted her in the air,
I looked at the dress she had to wear.
I put her down on the wooden deck,
She still looked beautiful to me,
Even though she was a wreck.
Then I looked into her eyes.
Then I gazed into the misty skies,
Suddenly a voice said 'Guard!'
Then they came in on me hard.
She then said 'He saved me,'
And turned to face the sea.
A man then said 'The boy's a hero!'
I no longer felt like a zero.
Footsteps gathered around the stern
Then I gave a crooked turn,
To that very special girl.

Colin Whittam (10)
Stourfield Junior School

SPARKY'S JOURNEY

S parky's the one who licks you like a slug and is snug as a rug.
P erhaps she is so small but you can't talk at all, she's the one
                                                      who loves us all.
A dog is the one who loves you best of all.
R un Sparky you're the one to fetch the ball.
K is for the kitten you love to play with.
Y es you can have a biscuit!
S parky you're a cheeky girl!

J ust a minute, only one biscuit!
O h dear, you've eaten two.
U nder the table you must go.
R ising behind the chair.
N ice girl Sparky.
E ar to ear you must cheer
Y es Sparky have a beer!

Claire McGrath (10)
Stourfield Junior School

MY SCARY JOURNEY

A plane is so big and scary,
Every time I am very wary.
Roll on the time I get off this plane,
Oh, by the way, my name's Wayne.
Please can you stop this, I am going to die,
Look over there, is that a fly?
Ah I feel very scared,
Now I wish I hadn't been dared.
Everyone seems calm and relaxed,
Scared and lonely I would rather pay my tax.

Paul Magookin (10)
Stourfield Junior School

THE CAR JOURNEY

T is for tears from the baby who doesn't want to go.
H is for the hiccups because the road is bumpy.
E is for the Earth moving round.

C is for the cassette player which we listen to.
A is for the aeroplane flying in the sky.
R is for the Rowntree's sweets we were eating.

J is for a joke my brother played on me.
O is for the oak tree we passed by.
U is for uncle Adrian who we're going to see.
R is for reading my book in the car.
N is for the nice new car.
E is for the exciting journey.
Y is for yes, we've arrived safely at last.

Rosanna Sly (9)
Stourfield Junior School

ADVENTURE

A key was lying on the ground
D efinately waiting to be found.
V ery still and very cold.
E ven though it was quite bold.
N ed that unfortunate chap,
T ook the key and never came back.
U nder the tree now he sits.
R elaxing his head in a pit.
E xperience tells us not to pick up strange keys, that will
      make you wobble at your knees.

Melissa Bailey (9)
Stourfield Junior School

A JOURNEY AROUND SCHOOL

Let's start the poem right away,
Start it now it won't take a day,
Early in the morning we go off to school,
When we go in we go in the hall.

After assembly we go into class,
Now it's science which involves some glass.
Next lesson it must be art,
Someone has just done a fart.

Now it's lunchtime, hip, hip, hooray!
But we've still got the rest of the day.
After lunch we go to play,
'Time to go in,' the teachers say.

Good! It's time to do PE
'Don't do that' she said to Lee.
All get into partners now,
Please do it without a row.

It's time for the last play of the day,
But we cannot get our own way.
The last lesson must be circle time,
Tomorrow I'm going to be nine!

Phew we can all go home,
And I can get my mobile phone.
I can just watch TV
I wonder what's on, let's go and see!

Sophie Ferguson (9)
Stourfield Junior School

THE TIME TRAVEL

Cuthbert the class swot,
Came up with a brilliant plot,
He made a time machine,
Told us where he'd been.
One by one we had a go,
To times that we did not know.

As soon as I stepped in the machine,
I wondered where the others had been.
I pressed the button, off we went,
To another world I was sent,
Whizzing through time, whizzing through space.
I was travelling to a different place.

In dinosaur times I left the machine,
Oh boy did those raptors look mean?
As pterodactyls circled above my head
I wished I was home in my warm bed.
A screeching noise, a terrifying yell,
There was trouble ahead, I could tell.

It was all very scary and not very pleasant,
I decided to travel back to the present,
In Cuthbert's machine I sped home,
Hoping and praying that I wasn't alone,
Didn't hear a noise, didn't hear a sound,
Until I was safely back on the ground.

Patrick Sullivan (10)
Stourfield Junior School

MY JOURNEY TO SUCCESS

When I went to Sydney it took twenty-odd hours,
I am a swimmer who is on a mission to get a medal.
When I get there it is down for business
Qualifying for the next round.
To get a medal for my country, Great Britain.
If I had a medal all the work would pay off.
Round after round I am getting more tired.
I can't believe it, I've made it to the final.
The day of the race I have butterflies in my stomach.
The crowds are cheering and flags are flying.
Everybody is silent as the starting gun fires
And the race is on.
I am determined to win the race,
So I swim harder than I have ever swam before.
I never look behind me, I just focus on the winning line,
The cheers are getting louder from the Great Britain corner.
I am the first to touch the edge of the pool.
I have finally won my goal – to win a gold medal,
The golden moment of my life.
Standing on the podium with the other medallists
I hear our national anthem God Save the Queen.
I can not hold back the tears of joy and pride
My journey has ended in success.

James Sumner (9)
Stourfield Junior School

A JOURNEY FROM THE PAST INTO THE FUTURE

A strange man came walking past,
That age didn't seem to last.
The Incas took out chickens' hearts,
And put them on donation carts.
The Egyptians buried their royals in tombs,
And made really pretty looms.
As for the Chinese I cannot say, for they really ate in a dirty way.
The Romans fought in war all day,
While servants made statues of Caesar from clay,
The Celts from Ireland were really nasty,
After battle they decided to party.
Elizabeth - a Tudor had a lot of heads cut off,
And lots of people at the time had a nasty cough.
Vile Victorians they really were,
Queen Victoria wore real fur.
In the 1900's cars were made,
But very little people got paid.
In the 1960's people began to dance,
And in the hospitals doctors poked and pranced -
Today, we still wonder -
Why children and grown-ups, are scared of loud thunder.

Abbey Murphy (10)
Stourfield Junior School

BLAST OFF!

I wanted to go into space,
To find a weird Martian race,
So I went to the rocket base.

I got inside the rocket,
With cakes stuffed in my pocket,
I also took off my locket.

I shot off to Mars,
Past the twinkling stars,
Next to cool space cars.

I took off to Jupiter
Where I met a Clupiter,
Nothing could be stupider.

Next I went to Saturn,
To buy a blue baton,
Aliens play badminton.

I hope I don't land in Rome,
I'd like some chocolate cake foam,
But I'm just happy I'm back home.

Kelly-Anne Conway (10)
Stourfield Junior School

THE GIRLS' DAY OUT

I'm on the boat,
I'm feeling sick,
Grab my coat,
We're leaving, quick!

Land ahoy! The anchor's down,
Come on girls, let's hit the town.
Oh my gosh what a meany,
My sister's got my best bikini.

It's getting dark,
The day is over,
Goodbye sharks,
Hello Dover.

Naomi Harvey (10)
Stourfield Junior School

MY VOYAGE TO SCHOOL

School is my favourite place,
It takes me five minutes to get there,
When the bell goes we all go in,
And start the lesson.

On my way to school,
I see lots of different things,
I count how many steps it takes me,
Today it was 104,
Tomorrow I'll try and get more.

On my way to school,
I call for my best friend,
Together we call for more,
I never go in the car, I always walk.

I play about in the playground,
When I'm waiting for the bell,
We go in at 10 to 9,
But I never want to,
When the bell goes for playtime I search for things.

And going home is the same,
But at home time,
I search for rocks.

Nicola Crawley (9)
Stourfield Junior School

JOURNEY UNDER THE SEA

I'm swimming under the ocean sea,
A group of seals swimming free,
They decided to flip and twirl over me,
I'm swimming under the ocean sea.

I'm swimming under the ocean sea,
A seahorse was swimming fast,
But he just swam straight past,
I'm swimming under the ocean sea.

I'm swimming under the ocean sea,
I saw a dolphin swimming by,
He squeaked out high,
I'm swimming under the sea.

I'm swimming under the ocean sea,
I saw a starfish,
I wouldn't like it on my dish,
I'm swimming under the ocean sea.

I've got out of the ocean sea,
To have my lovely tea.

Sophie Lankester (9)
Stourfield Junior School

RUN TO THE DISCO

On to the disco,
I must walk,
On to the disco,
No foul talk,

I dance, I prance,
I sing, I eat,
I dance, I prance,
Discos are a treat.

Stephanie Roy (9)
Stourfield Junior School

MY MOTORBIKE

Feel the revs of my bike,
It's a two wheeler not a trike.

Dressed in leather, safety first.
I need to ride, adrenaline burst.

Feather the clutch, hold on tight.
Full speed, wheelies, fantastic fright.

Here we are on the beach,
To the others we are out of reach.

Petrol needed and new tyres,
Cool the engine, before she fires.

I need a sleep, I feel so weak,
Where shall I lay to end this day?

Energy thirst, pull the throttle back,
Must hit the road and get back on track.

Reach for the stars within my grasp,
I have arrived; I am here at last.

Ryan Carter (9)
Stourfield Junior School

THE SMUGGLER'S JOURNEY

Smuggler is on a journey,
He really needs his cloak,
Smuggler is on a journey,
He's not that bad a bloke.
So now he's on his horse
And off he goes of course.
Oh my word, his horse is tired!
He must get there or he'll be fired.
So now he is at the coast,
His horse is resting near a post.
There is the boat to get to Spain,
He's on his journey once again.

Now he is back on land,
He's got a gun in his hand!
But now he's got to walk in Spain
He's off on his journey once again.

Jamie Roe (9)
Stourfield Junior School

THE GROOVY GIRL

I am walking down the street
Like a fashionable girl
With a very nice beat
And I do lots of twirls.

I am pretty
I am lovely
And my hair is in a curl
I am a lovely dovely girl.

Now I am at the party
You can come and party too
I saw a boy called Barty
Boo to you too!

Jade Hall (9)
Stourfield Junior School

MY TRAIN JOURNEY

I found my tickets, I'm on the train,
A man nearly hit me with his cane.
Now I am sat on this seat,
Just about to rest my feet,
I met a couple of friendly blokes,
They told me lots of funny jokes.
They said to me 'We're off right now',
Then I passed a cow.
Then I saw a little boy,
Playing with his new train toy.
It had plastic wheels and a steel tin top,
Off flew the roof with a big loud pop.
The boy cried loudly for his mummy,
From his stomach came something funny,
A big loud rumble for something yummy.
I've just got off at somewhere called Reading
I've got to find some new bedding.
Now I'm opening my front door,
I've just dropped my keys on the floor.

Lauren Miller (9)
Stourfield Junior School

MY JOURNEY THROUGH SPACE

I'm on a mission to space.
To find alien life!
People have been reporting strange things.
Each night at 1am.
So we're trying to find intelligent life in space.
Our spaceship is made out of steel
And is called Cruise.
We are in space trying to find life.
We've been past Mars. What? There's an alien spaceship.
'Alien alert, alien alert', says the signal.
But that says 'Apollo', oops.
Now we've been past Saturn, Jupiter, Neptune, Uranus and Pluto.
But because the stars were so bright
We were forced to go back to Earth
So are aliens, aliens out there?
No one knows.

Jake Harvey (9)
Stourfield Junior School

THE FUTURE POEM

Zooming on my blades,
With the wind in my hair
I suddenly travel back in time
And meet Tony Blair.

Whizzing on my bike
While flying through the air
Trying to eat my apple pie
Now I'm really scared.

Blasting in my rocket
It's all about to end
'Cause when I get to Mars
I'll probably go round the bend!

Nicholas Benavidez (9)
Stourfield Junior School

FOREVER FRIENDS

Every single step you take, it will never break.
We will all hold the world in our hands until night breaks up the lands.
We have joy, we have fun, we have seasons in the sun,
But the joy that we had is now gone.
We're friends, friends, forever friends.
We sang lots of songs, really funny songs.
We play and play all day.
We sing, dance, clap or play all day forever.
Ouch, now that hurt.
I'm not your friend in the band any longer,
Because we are longer, stronger.
I want you to stay for ever,
I don't know what to do every day every night.
All the time we have a fright.
Girls, we're friends, we're friends,
We don't even step on each other's toes
Oh we're so happy,
Going to live forever
Baby we're so happy,
Cos we're friends forever.

Kristy Legg (8)
Stourfield Junior School

MY VOYAGE THROUGH SPACE

We were launched at 05:00 hours
In a shuttle that was ours.
It was a pretty rough ride,
And the rest of the crew died.

So I looked out the window and out into the sky
And when I looked out I was very surprised.
What I saw was very odd because it was the Star Trek Enterprise.
But I looked again and I was face to face with an alien that said 'Hi'.
I shouted, 'Houston, I'm a problematic'
'Why?' they said
'Because I'm asthmatic.'
I shouted 'I'm coming in to land.'
I crashed and fell into some sand.

Harry Lund (10)
Stourfield Junior School

THE FLOAT

Today we're getting ready,
The flight is coming soon,
The balloon is so, so steady,
I see the sparkling moon.

I slide into the basket,
That's woven with a willow,
Now this ride has no ticket,
Nor a comfy pillow.

I'm drifting through the air,
I feel like a weightless stone,
Over at reality I stare,
Now I'm going home alone.

Karen Hawey (10)
Stourfield Junior School

JAMES AND THE GIANT SKITTLE

When James was little
he got eaten by a giant skittle.
When he was inside
he really wanted to be outside.
By the time he saw someone
they really hadn't gone one to one.
They said 'Hey, what's your name?
you're really not the same.'
We sailed to China,
Then to Italy and France,
where we stopped to have a dance.
We went to the moon and back
but after all of that we had a little idea.
We went back to my front door scared
my wicked aunts, so we got out the skittle,
went inside, there on the table was another giant skittle.

Alex Winston (10)
Stourfield Junior School

MY SPACE MISSION

Here I am stuck in a rocket ship,
I'm eating an apple, just swallowed the pip.
I'm in the dark all alone,
I wish right now I was at home.
I'm on my way to space right now,
I just bumped into a moo, moo cow!
The cow was jumping over the moon,
He said to me he'll be back very soon!

Zoe Stanley (9)
Stourfield Junior School

MY VOYAGE TO REDISCOVER THE TITANIC

With all my knowledge about the Titanic,
I decided to rediscover it.
So I borrowed a boat and got some scuba gear
And set off to the Atlantic Ocean for at least a year.

It was so cold I could not feel my feet,
Or hear my heart beat!
I got into my gear
And I started to fear
That I would not come back for another year.

Now I'm down in the ocean,
And I had some emotion,
Now I'm swimming to the wreck,
And I'm going to the deck.

The ship's deck is really big,
It would be hard to dig,
Now I'm going to go back up,
I think I've had some luck.

Now I'm back on the boat,
And my throat sounds like a goat!
Now I'm out of my gear
I'm going home for another year.

Adam Chastney (10)
Stourfield Junior School

THE PLANE JOURNEY THAT WENT WRONG

I was going on holiday to Sweden,
And hoped to get a swede.
The pilot's name was Adam,
And thought he was a bad 'un.
He met a fairy, a bad one too,
The bad one had a cow, moo moo.
She put a curse on Adam and the cow,
And he's going to roast just about now.
He started going mad,
And made the cow feel sad.
On the plane the next day,
I heard Adam say,
'I feel like I'm in Heaven,'
But really he's in Devon.
Five, four, three, two, one,
Uh oh, something's gone wrong.
We're not moving,
But it does feel soothing,
Four seconds later, 'Blast off!' said a voice,
Just then there was lots of noise.
The plane was above,
A blackbird and a dove.
I never knew what went wrong,
To me it just dropped a couple of thousand feet
The pilot said that the engine went.

Gina Legg (10)
Stourfield Junior School

THE BIKE JOURNEY

T he riding has just begun now,
H e started the bike and went over the mountains high and low,
E ating a burger on the way, he started to get so slow.

B iking as fast as he could,
I nto the mountains then into the woods.
K icking the pedals as fast as he could,
E xpecting to see his mother, as he would.

J am and cookies from Mum,
O ver the tall mountains, chewing his gum.
U ntucking his umbrella from his jacket to stop the rain.
R ain chucking down and he started to get a bit of a pain.
N ow he's nearly there,
E ating another cookie, now he's there.
Y es Mum, I'm here.

Liam Colebourn (10)
Stourfield Junior School

VAMPIRE FOOTSTEPS

Vampire footsteps in the hallway,
The heavy doorway creaks open wide,
A creepy voice out of nowhere,
'Step this way, do come inside.'

Candles flicker in the darkness,
A floating lantern leads the way,
Down silent hall and empty passage,
Cold draughts blow and shadows play.

Cobwebs stretch from every corner,
Black bats with gingery cats,
Portraits watch as you creep by them,
On the floor run squeaking rats.

The lantern glows in the great hall,
Dimly lit by candle light,
Empty but for one large coffin -
What a dreaded, fearful sight!

Lewis Gilbert & Ziad Alazhar (10)
Stourfield Junior School

ALONE AT SEA

The ship has crashed, it's deadly too,
I'm all alone without the crew.
I swim to the shore,
Ooh! A crab's claw.
I lay on the sand,
With head in hand,
I had a dream,
A total scream,
Whenever I spoke,
I get the poke,
All because I had,
A bachelor pad.
But I'd rather not be,
All alone at sea.
I'd rather have a pad,
In hot Trinidad.

Simon Challis (9)
Stourfield Junior School

The Endless Run

Fast as a lion
Quick as a fox

    I'm running so fast
    I'm losing my socks!

        Fast as a cheetah
        Quick as a rat

            I'm running so fast
            I'm losing my hat!

                Fast as a rocket
                Quick as a hare

                    I'm running so fast
                    I'm losing my hair!

                        Fast as a car
                        Quick as a mare

                              I'm running so fast
                              I'm getting nowhere!

Rory Lucas (10)
Stourfield Junior School

The Voyage Through Sunset

Leisurely pedalling up the steep hill,
On one sweltering sunny day,
Starting to feel a bit under the weather,
The sky was blue as the luscious blue heather.

Moonlight had come and the sun had gone down,
Children were running so I knew it was near town,
I'd been cycling for ages and I felt pale,
When I got to the top of the hill I felt well.

Stephanie Gibbons & Roseanna Blackshaw (9)
Stourfield Junior School

Yellow Submarine

It's better than you've ever seen,
In my yellow submarine.
You see fishes and of course whales,
Little sharks with big tails.
Can't stop now, we've got to go faster!
We start to scream at our poor master.
'Come on, you're awfully slow,
About as slow as my gran Mo!'
Don't stop now, there's more to see,
Don-don fish and caterpie.
Octopus and shovel fish,
Catch one of those, it'll give you a wish.
'What? That's strange, we're slowing down.'
'Of course we are, you silly clown.
It's the end of the ride.'
'Wow! That was cool' I sighed.
'Goodbye now, I must go!
I must see my old gran Mo!'

Adam Watt (10)
Stourfield Junior School

JOURNEY OF MY FEARS

They're colourful,
They're horrible!
They have big, black, beady eyes.
Under the sea,
As mean as can be,
They have big, black, beady eyes,
They're slimy,
They're scaly,
They have big, black, beady eyes!

I'm off the boat,
Don't need a float!
Just on Pearl Island,
My cottage has a pool,
It's really cool,
Just on Pearl Island,
It also has a pond,
I need a magic wand,
Just on Pearl Island!

I went on an adventure,
With my brother!
I'm on a quest to get off Pearl Island,
My fear is multiplying,
'Cause I've just seen a fish flying,
I'm on a quest to get off Pearl Island,
I want to go home,
I need to use the phone,
I'm on a quest to get off Pearl Island!

I met a peasant,
Who had a pet pheasant!
Pearl Island is really scary,
I thought I saw a zombie,
But it was just a man named Pombie,
Pearl Island is really scary,
I found some quicksand,
But I managed to stay on land,
Pearl Island is really scary!

I really wish,
I was back with the fish!
My fears are better than this,
I don't care if slimy, scaly,
Anything really,
My fears are better than this.
I made a friend that offered me food,
But my mum said that was rude,
My fears are better than this!

This holiday stinks!

Hannah Godwin (9)
Stourfield Junior School

JOURNEY TO EARTH

There once was a boy
Who travelled in space
He rode his jet booster
All over the place
And then one day
He saw a star
Shining brightly from afar
He put some fuel in his jet booster
To get closer to the star
But when he got there
It was so bright
He couldn't tell if it was day or night
But behind this star hid a beautiful planet
There it was, Earth.

Kyle Freeman (9)
Stourfield Junior School

THE DROP

Here I am with my parachute,
Up above the ground so high,
Here I am with my parachute,
On goes the green light.
Out I jump,
With a bump!
I'm gliding down like a bird,
Just then I couldn't speak a word,
I pull the string
I lose my ring,
I touch the ground,
And don't make a sound.

Ross Hawey (10)
Stourfield Junior School